Weaving Profits

How To Make Money Selling Your Handwovens or Any Other Crafts

by James Dillehay

Warm Snow
Publishers

ISBN 0-9629923-9-9

Library of Congress Catalog Card No. 91-065855

Warm Snow Publishers
PO Box 75
Torreon, NM 87061

Preface

The happiest people do what they love regardless of how it will turn out or much money they will make. If you're reading this book you have at least flirted with the idea of self employment from your weaving or craft knowledge. I started writing *Weaving Profits* because of the pain, frustrations and losses of my early days in business and realized that the negative experiences still hurt. I felt that if I could present what I learned from my experiences to others, it would make their way a little easier. This is the intention behind this book, to ease your way to having your own business selling your handmade products.

I had another motivation as well in producing this book. You might call it revenge of a sort. Revenge against the dehumanizing policies of corporate or big business employment. Many of us are getting more and more frustrated with working for large companies for little pay where the policy is always "TIME EQUALS MONEY." The problem for the workers is that *its their time and their life that equals the corporations' money.*

This is true for all employees, no matter what level. I left a secure position as vice president of a chain of retail career clothing stores in Texas because it did not satisfy any deeper needs. I created nothing excepting paperwork and sales of several other companys' products without any personal connection or interest in what was being sold or how it was made. I didn't know what I would end up doing when I left, but I knew I would only be happy when I could make a living with my own hands selling something I created. Soon I learned to weave and started selling my work through many of the ideas presented in *Weaving Profits*.

Caution; it's easier to start a business than it is to keep one going; most new businesses fail within the first three to five years because of inadequate planning and insufficient capital. How do you know if you have what it takes to beat the odds? The aspiring weaver or entrepreneur must grasp the important difference between "wish" and "hope". Wishing for success in business or anything else will almost certainly guarantee your failure. It is the immature person's efforts to impose fantasy on reality.

Hope, on the other hand, is based on efforts and reality testing. Like a gardener, you clear the earth, plant seeds, feed and protect young plants and hope that nature will take its course. But your efforts will make the successful harvest, not your "wishing". With that in mind, I have presented a great many useful tools to help your business start and grow. If my advice helps you in some way or you have some interesting experiences of your own to tell, please write me care of the publisher's address on the copyright page. Best of luck.

J.D.

Table of Contents

Introduction

Opportunities for selling handwoven and other craft products are many, but an artisan must first learn to focus their energies on a manageable target or risk loosing valuable time and resources trying to do too many things at once.

The best approach is to start selling your work to friends and relatives and see what they like best. When you have produced a large enough inventory of different pieces, try a local arts and crafts show. From doing several shows, you'll quickly learn which products sell best. Store owners approach craftspeople at most of the larger craft shows. If you want to sell to stores, there is plenty of advice in Chapter 5.

As you read through this book, you will find more and more ways to sell your products. Don't be discouraged by the immensity of it all. You can make your business a part-time venture or build it into a large, full-scale operation. Remember though, one step at a time.

I'm probably guilty of that natural tendency to want to help others avoid making the same mistakes I did. I burned myself often, but I always learned something. *Weaving Profits* shows you how to save yourself some of this pain and make more money. I just hope my advice doesn't sound too much like the ten commandments of a craft business.

"Thou shalt not commit replication *(unless it pays)* . . . Thou shalt not kill employees who screw up . . .Thou shalt not covet thy neighbor's designs. . . Thou shalt not undercut thy wholesale accounts in the same city . . ."

My hope is that the ideas you find here will help you accomplish these four things: 1) fire your passion to plan your own destiny, 2) help you gain the financial independence that gives you time to create great masterpieces, 3) become the richest person on your block, and 4) take enough time to spend the night with your spouse occasionally. Best of luck on that one.

I smile now at my own early ambitions. My first weaving project was a sampler scarf. The draft was a mix of patterns; colors grouped randomly in the warp. For the weft, I sometimes followed a treadling my teacher gave me, sometimes I struck out on my own. I threw in the weft yarns wildly, without regard for compatible fibers. Somewhere in my mind's eye, untamed visions of siren colors battled one another for expression. Speeding onward, I wove in a fever fed by whirlwind hopes. On, on, on, weaving toward promises of the most stunning textile vision in the state . . . no, the whole world . . . no, no, throughout all time . . .
and then, somehow, finished, it didn't quite look like this piece was going to get me on the Donahue Show after all.

My friend Adnan walked in the weaving room just as I was cutting the piece from the loom. After I finished, all I wanted to do was get it off the loom and out of my sight. I told him I was going to wrap it around my bench as a seat cushion. But he complimented it, saying no, you should sell it, someone will love this. I doubted it.

A few days later, another friend, Janet, visiting the area from New York, walked by my loom and saw the scarf where I had draped it over the castle. She fell in love. She wanted to buy the scarf, but I had no idea how much to charge. Meekly, I said "how about $20." She said OK, and that was the start of my business. $20 for a siren vision.

Later, Janet asked me to make her a shawl. Then, another scarf. Then, a few for gifts. Then, her boyfriend Tom wanted something for her. My first few months went like that, yielding a series of friendly commissions, learning experiences, and enough money to pay the bills.

There's plenty of advice in these pages on all aspects of starting and expanding your business, but there's one element that plays a bigger role in your success than any other; the use of color. Color is the life in weaving or almost any craft medium. The choice of color is the biggest reason people buy any handwoven piece.

Don't be shy, use colors as if you were a millionaire throwing dollar bills to the people. Be generous in your creations and the buying public will reward you. Always listen to what customers say about your work, but be aware, success will come from noticing what they buy.

Section 1

How To Start Without Falling on Your Face
or
Learn to Walk First, Maybe You Won't Need to Run Later

Chapter 1   Wondering What Sells?

Start small. Many persons try to start their business at the top. They then proceed to work their way quickly to the bottom. If you take on simple things first and do them well, the bigger tasks come by themselves.

Where do you begin? You may have already learned there's no problem in finding ideas of projects to make. The challenge is to find craft products that the public wants to buy and deciding whether you want to make them. For every artist or craftsperson in business, marketing their work becomes a constant wrestling match between the forces of creating and selling.

Gathering ideas

So how do you find out what the public wants? First, look for examples of what consumers are buying at the crafts fairs. I was fortunate to begin my weaving education with a weaver/artist who had been selling her work at shows for some years. She wove garments using colors and designs inspired from her years as an artist. Her line of clothing sold well and provided her with a regular income.

Your weaver's or craft guild may have at least one member that makes a living from selling their work. Also, talk with weavers at craft shows. I found more than half the weavers I met at craft shows to be friendly and surprisingly open about their business, though some weren't. One weaver asked me if I'd leave town; I said "no." That was the end of the conversation. So, try somebody else. It can't hurt to ask.

Second, see what's selling in retail stores. Most store owners, when they aren't busy, are anxious to talk about what moves well and what doesn't. Ask them what sells in their store. If you tell them your in the business, you might even get your first order this way.

Third, look for inspiration of product ideas (don't blindly copy them) in magazines like *Handwoven, FiberArts, Shuttle Spindle & Dyepot, Ornament* and *Weavers*. Most all crafts have at least one magazine devoted to the field. The library's periodical section can help you.

Fourth, you have still another resource to check out; your own creativity. Look at other people's work only for inspiration, not as a substitute for work and the joy of producing unique pieces. You'll find no pleasure, and more grief, in blatantly copying another artisan's workmanship. I rarely see other weavers making pieces exactly like mine. In fact, at some shows with twelve to fifteen weavers exhibiting, I have found that most often, the work was distinctly different.

It's a free marketplace out there. If you want to make a place for yourself, work for it. You have the same creative spark that everyone else has. Find yours and go for it. The connection between an artist and her creation is more than vanity. This is the reality of creative energy. It has force and power to attract.

To make the whole craft business thing work, you must compromise. Part of your time, you spend working with the creative energy. Part of your time, you try to make a few bucks. The rest of your time you shouldn't spend thinking about the other two times.

Even if you aren't a creative genius you can still prosper. You can make your work appear desirable in the eyes of your customer by learning the different reasons involved in what motivates humans to buy. This chapter is about those elements.

Who is going to buy your work?

Somebody will, but figuring out who that someone is can cost you time and money when you're first starting out. To avoid the guessing, it helps to list the groups that have an interest in your product. Call these groups 'broad market categories or areas of potential sales. An example of a list might include:
1) Home, 2) Clothing, 3) Accessories, 4) Interior design, 5) Art, 6) Toys, 7) Textile industry, 8) Special occasion, 9) Religious, 10) Jewelry, 11) Other

After you have come up with a list of the different groups, think about all the different items that could be sold to each market. Following is an example of lists of products that fit under the various broad market categories. These lists show a few handwoven items that the public buys with space provided to write in your own ideas. A list like this gives you a clear picture of what's possible and practical, in terms of making and selling handwovens. Note that the order in which the items appear on this sample list does not reflect their sales, ease of production or profitability. We will look at those elements later.

Fig. 1.0 Broad market categories with list of products for each

Home	placemats, table runners, napkins, curtains, towels, table cloths, fire screens, baskets, pillows, blankets, room dividers, coverlets, throws, wall hangings, mantle covers, floor rugs
Clothing	cocoons, shawls, blouses, dresses, suits, quetchmetls, kimonos, fichus (triangular shawl), men's and women's: shirts, vests, ruanas, sweaters, jackets, coats
Accessories	handbags, purses, belts, sashes, babushkas, mittens, mufflers, house slippers, boas, men's: cummerbunds, cravats, bow ties, men's and women's: scarves, hats, caps, tams, bandannas, ties
Interior design	wall hangings, rugs, upholstery fabric, throws, curtains, passementeries, pillows, room dividers, screens, fabric trim
Art	rugs, tapestries, wall hangings, woven sculpture, paper weaving or other media

Toys	stuffed toys, dolls, puppets
Textile industry	samples for fabric industry, fabric by the yard
Special occasion	wedding gowns and shawls, baby blankets, greeting card inserts, Christmas ornaments, stockings, Easter bunnies, heart pillows for Valentine's day
Religious	altar objects, vestments, tapestries, chalice palls, baptismal towels, banners, chasubles, stoles
Woven jewelry	earrings, bracelets, necklaces, rings, anklets, headbands
Other	tote bags, duffel bags, backpacks, garment bags; fabric for antique furniture and autos; saddle-blankets, halters; fabric for other weavers; reweaving or restoration

That's over 100 possible items, counting men's and women's garments separately. There is no likelihood that you could sanely or competently produce work for more than a few of these categories without employing others to help. For a one-person shop, it's more reasonable to concentrate on one or two markets and a spread of products aimed at each group.

The secret to winning the marketing game is to channel your energies and resources toward the group(s) of purchasers most likely to buy your hand-woven products. If you try to make too many different items, or try to sell to those who don't want your products, you dissipate your momentum, end up broke, and say to heck with the whole business.

Find a few things that sell well and concentrate on building a bread and butter line. Make products that sell steadily so you can earn the money to stay in business from month to month. Once you have established that wonderful menu of income-producing products, you can explore the possibilities of other types of weaving, perhaps more one-of-a-kind pieces.

Or, maybe you'll keep expanding the production lines. If you're good at delegating work, you can hire others to sew, produce or sell for you. At least by the time increased sales force you to decide, you'll have the financial freedom to choose.

Sales vehicles

No, this isn't about used cars. Sales vehicles are the ways you approach your markets. You have a list of markets and products. Now write down all the possible ways to reach each group. Suppose you want to know at a glance how many ways are there to sell woven jewelry? Look at this example:

Fig. 1.1 Vehicles to sell your products

Category	Item	Selling Vehicle
Woven jewelry	earrings	craft shows, renaissance shows, mall shows, direct to stores, sales reps, mail order, catalogs, gift trade shows, other trade shows, county and state fairs, studio sales, co-operative galleries, home parties, door-to-door (any other ideas?)

Make a market list every product you have thought of weaving. Which products offer the most opportunities for sales? Keep these lists and add new ideas as your experience grows.

You may suspect that many products in Figure 1.0 might not have a large enough market to turn a profit. This is true. But how can you know ahead of time? Several influences affect a product's saleablility. Look at your product ideas in relation to the elements that follow.

What is your product's function?

The first question to ask yourself is what will the item be used for? Does it have a function that makes it useful to a person in daily life? Does it fill a basic human need? Or, will the piece be sold as decorative art, like sculpture or painting? Think of the work as either being functional, or art. (Please, no arguments about art's aesthetic function).

Elements affecting product sales include:
item's function
geographic location
demographics
seasons
wholesale or retail?

Why does it make a difference? The reason is that everyone has needs. They will buy something they can use before they buy a piece of art. Also, they will buy something they can wear before they buy a piece of furniture. And, they will usually buy something to eat before they buy clothing.

Basic human motivations

The well known humanistic psychologist, Dr. Abraham Maslow developed a theory of human motivation that says that everyone is motivated by a set of needs and that these needs can be classified into various levels of importance.

The first level is our physiological needs; those are for food, drink, sleep, exercise and so on. The second level is our safety or security needs; protection against threat, danger or deprivation. Level three is our social needs; that is the need for belonging, acceptance, love and friendship. Level four, sometimes called ego needs; refers to the need for self confidence, achievement, status, recognition, and respect for others. Level five is self fulfillment; the need to realize one's potential, to create, and to experience personal growth and peak experiences.

Once a person satisfies a need, that need no longer motivates them, but, if a need is frustrated, it becomes important. By looking at the function of a product or promotional idea in view of this theory, you can see how a customer's buying priorities will be arranged. Does your product fill one or more of these needs?

It might help to translate some of these levels into more general terms like freedom from fear, health, emotional comfort, more money, being popular, convenience, entertainment, someone to love, time, sexual fulfillment, pride, physical comfort and attractiveness, prestige and so on. Evaluate your products against the list and see if they help meet any of the basic needs. A

Fig. 1.2 Maslow's hierarchy of needs

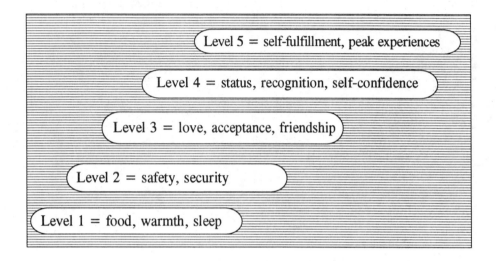

handwoven bedspread might keep you warm, be attractive to look at, have value as an heirloom, be worthy of pride, a subject of entertaining conversation, or be convenient to use.

Most new products fail when introduced into the marketplace because they lack familiarity. (Let's exclude technological products like computers). This is because when a person feels threatened or uncomfortable, it impinges on the important basic needs for safety or security. Often, something new or unheard of, raises doubt or subtle anxiety. But take an item that assures the customer of time proven use and durability, add a new twist or design element, and you have a winner.

Certain handcrafted items have survived the test of time in all of the world's marketplaces. Wherever archeologists uncover ruins, they always seem to find jewelry, pottery, inlays, bits of weavings, and other crafts. Back then, everything was handmade. Now, people consider handcrafted work a collectible novelty.

There is another need that is typically American and equally important to know about. You can see the evidence of it at any good crafts show. We are part of a consumer society. People feel a need to spend money. Otherwise, they don't feel connected to their social and cultural environment. They're going to spend money anyway, so it might as well be with you.

Geographic location

Location affects the sales of many items. Geography influences woven goods used in the home like rag rugs and placemats less than clothing. For instance, you probably won't sell as many scarves in Phoenix and San Diego as you will in Boston, New York, or Chicago. Placemats, on the other hand, may be found in homes everywhere. Sometimes, locational marketing can be tricky. You might think that horse saddle blankets wouldn't do well in New York City, yet throroughbred horse shows are well attended there.

If your product has nationwide appeal, you can plan sales efforts on a big scale. But, just because an item sells only to a specific area of the country, it isn't necessarily a handicap. You can get excellent results by targeting specific geographical interest groups. In any case, focusing on your audience's particular needs is the key to using your resources more effectively.

Demographics

Demographics are elements like age, sex, family style, occupation, income and religion. For instance, if you make handwoven dolls, your largest group of customers will be parents and relatives of children. If you make tapestries with religious images, your sales efforts will be directed to church groups. Obviously, an item that appeals to the most groups will have the biggest sales.

If woven jewelry is your line, most of your sales will be to women. In fact, women are the largest group of consumers for any products. This is true for home items as well as clothing and other woven pieces. Remember this when you design your displays or write promotional material.

Season

Seasons influence some items more than others, like location. Some products can be marketed only at certain times of the year. Clothing sales are the most seasonal while home and office item sales follow normal retail selling trends throughout the year. For most products, you can expect to do half or more of your annual business from fall through Christmas. These are the months for biggest retail sales.

Greeting cards with woven inserts lend themselves well to seasonal and holiday buying. Valentine's and Mother's Days are excellent examples. Any low priced piece with hearts in the design will sell because customers don't hesitate to spend a couple of dollars to say 'I love you' to a friend or sweetheart. They are a perfect gift item at an inexpensive price. And don't forget Christmas, Hanukkah and Easter.

Wholesale or retail?

Will you sell your product wholesale to stores? Or will you sell retail at craft shows, boutiques and mail order? What if you want to do both? At first, you can only guess which of your products will do best in any given market. Later, by keeping track of sales, you can see how some pieces will not work at crafts shows, yet sell excellently in stores and galleries.

Overlapping effects

Often you will find variables overlapping each other's influence. For instance, if you weave, knit or sew sweaters, the obvious place for better sales would be states where the weather is cooler. But, you might find a craft show in Florida or Arizona with vacationing 'snow birds' (tourists from the northern states who go south for the winter) who will buy your sweaters to take back north. You could receive orders from wholesale accounts in April or May for these same sweaters for August delivery, though sweaters are thought of as fall or winter merchandise.

Fig. 1.3 Table of variables influencing product sales.

	Products				
Variables	Rag rug	Placemat	Shawl	Wall hanging	Saddle blanket
Function/ Need	1	1	2	1	1
Geographic location	5	6	4	6	3
Season	4	4	2	4	2
Demographic	4	2	2	3	1
Wholesale/ retail	2	2	2	2	1
Total	16	15	12	15	8

Fig. 1.4 Overlapping variables

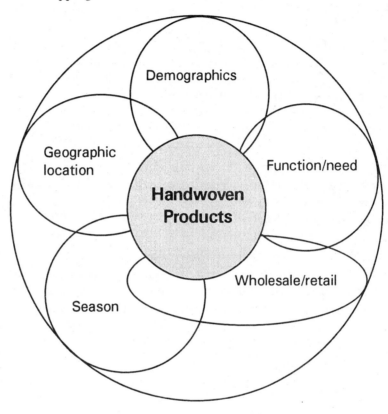

Understand the variables. Plan ahead to take advantage of prime opportunities. Any craftsperson's business would benefit from considering the above mentioned elements.

How to decide

With so many considerations, everything may look a bit confusing by now. A bigger picture helps. Figure 1.3 shows a example chart to use in helping learn how product sales are influenced by the variables mentioned.

Assign a set of number values to each element that influences a product's sales potential. Every variable can be assigned a value of one point. For example, there are four seasons, so if a product can be sold in all four seasons, it receives a value of 4 under the Season column. In this example, geographic influences are 1 to 6 (the northeast, the southeast, the upper Midwest, the south, the northwest, and the west). Demographics are the components like sex, age, family style, job, religion and income level. If an item can be sold either wholesale or retail it gets a 1; for both, it gets a 2.

The items with the highest totals in your charts will be the products or markets easiest to generate sales from because they appeal to the widest audience. You can add other influential criteria to the chart as you think of them. However good charts and figures might look on paper, they're only a visual aid to give perspective to the choices facing you. Decisions will change with experience, instincts and the state of your resources.

Even with the most detailed calculation and years of selling experience, you can only second guess the public's buying whims or any other elements beyond your control. The information presented here is an adjunct to good old intuition, not as a substitute.

The original title of this chapter was: Wondering What Sells? How About Mohair Shorts? This started as a joke between another weaver and myself about what she should make for her boyfriend's birthday. You may, or may not think the idea of selling mohair shorts is amusing, but consider this: how often do customers buy unusual gifts as a joke? A lot. Sometimes the weirder the idea, the more appeal it has. If anyone tries this idea, let me know how it goes, I'm itching to find out.

Chapter 2 I'm Afraid to Charge for My Work, Can't I Just Give it Away?

Of course you can give your things away! I found myself doing this for months before I realized what I was doing.

Most beginning craftspeople are shy about charging enough for their work, but if you intend to stay in business longer than three to four months, you need to take a good look at how much you're asking for your work and how you came to this decision.

Will you sell wholesale, retail, or both?

Wholesale means selling to someone, who in turn, marks up the price and sells the items to the public. Examples are stores, galleries, and catalog companies. Retail means you sell your work direct to the public as at arts and crafts shows, home parties, by mail order, or from your studio or retail store. There is no reason to restrict yourself to one or the other, unless you want to. Many craftspeople do business at both levels. It isn't difficult, just keep the distinction between the two pricing schedules clear.

Store owners want to work with someone who conveys a professional attitude. This includes having price lists, brochures and order forms with clearly explained prices and terms ready to hand out upon request.

Always have prices on hang tags on every piece. Neglecting to price your work at craft shows doesn't pay. Most shoppers get irritated when they can't find a price tag on an item. A voice in their mind is asking if you're charging the same to everyone.

Here's another common situation that arises at craft shows. You're doing just fine selling pieces. Everyone likes your work, including someone who suddenly appears and asks if you wholesale your work to stores. She wants prices, your payment terms and when you can deliver. Are you ready with the answers? If you are unprepared, this situation can put you off balance and you could easily lose a possible outlet for your work. This chapter helps you find exactly how much to charge in either wholesale or retail environments.

Average market price

At first, I was uncomfortable pricing my work as high as other weavers. Because I lacked confidence in my creations, I was settling for lower income. It was not long before I became painfully aware of the need for getting full dollar value for my efforts. Looking at my expenses incurred from the shows, my labor, and my overhead, I found I was producing high quality weaving for much less than minimum wage.

One solution for anyone starting out is to go around to several craft shows and check the prices that similar handwoven items are selling for.

Check prices for the same items in stores and galleries as well. You can figure that your price to the store will be 50% of what they charge to the public. Note that the prices will differ in a retail store and in a craft show for the same item. For handwovens, the store price is usually higher. Keep this in mind when pricing your pieces.

Don't let lack of experience prevent you from asking equivalent prices for your work *if it is of equal quality* to that of your competition. You can't go wrong if you stick close to what everyone else is asking.

At craft shows, you will encounter the time-honored tradition of bargaining. You can make use of this by knowing the floor price of your work, discussed below. Then, you can build in a 10 or 15% bargaining amount to your prices. At good shows, I have taken in as much as $400 or more near the end when customers come around to look for last minute deals as we are packing up to go home.

The average market price for similar work is also called the ceiling price. This is the most you should charge for your weaving in similar outlets. If you exceed the ceiling price by too much, your sales will suffer. If you charge much less, the same could happen because you have 'cheapened' the value of the piece.

You could use the ceiling amount as a pricing strategy indefinitely. If you only intend to do craft shows, all you ever need to know is how much the average customer is willing to pay for a product.

On the other hand, if your sales are high but you aren't making a profit, you need to find exactly what it costs you to make a piece and to sell it. Knowing that, you can then make intelligent choices as whether to stop producing unprofitable items or find ways to make them at lower cost.

Floor price

For every top, somewhere there's a bottom. While the average market price for your products is the ceiling price, or the most you will charge, the formulas below will give you the floor price, the lowest price you can safely charge for an item and insure a fair profit.

> Ceiling price = the average market price of similar work
>
> Floor price = production cost + cost of sales
>
> Production cost = indirect costs + labor + materials

To find the floor price of your work, you must learn the production cost, or what it costs to make an item, plus what it costs to sell it. Production cost is the sum of your indirect costs, labor costs and materials costs. Following is an explanation of what these expenses are. Figuring the cost of sales is covered afterwards.

Indirect costs

Indirect costs are those expenses necessary to keep your business running daily. These include rent, utilities, travel expenses, insurance and so on. Your first year in business, you'll probably have to guess at these costs. There's no way to know what your indirect costs will be without paying bills over time. Nevertheless, within the first six months, you should have a good idea of the money you spend to keep things going.

An example in Figure 2.1 shows a list of indirect costs by the month and by the year. Here, the total expenses for the year is $9,960. Some of your expenses like travel, advertising, or shipping costs will vary from month to month. This makes it more practical to project an entire year's costs because

Fig. 2.1 Sample of indirect costs.

Expenses	Per month	Per year
rent	$250	$3,000
utilities	$ 50	$ 600
show fees	$200	$2,400
travel	$ 60	$ 720
depreciation	$ 10	$ 120
services	$ 15	$ 180
transportation	$ 50	$ 600
insurance	$ 50	$ 600
postage & UPS	$ 15	$ 180
telephone	$ 40	$ 480
advertising	$ 25	$ 300
interest & bank fees	$ 30	$ 360
office supplies	$ 10	$ 120
miscellaneous	$ 25	$ 300
	$830	$9,960

by the end of 12 months, you will have gone through a complete cycle of expenses.

Even if you don't intend to do your own taxes, it's important that you familiarize yourself with all the possible deductions allowed by the IRS. Tax laws change frequently. A certified public accountant (C.P.A.) will be aware of the latest changes in these laws. A superior guide for small businesses has been written by Bernard Kamaroff, C.P.A., titled *Small Time Operator: How To Start Your Own Business, Keep Your Books, Pay Your Taxes, And Stay Out Of Trouble*. This manual contains all the details of setting up a business from scratch. There are many charts and examples of record keeping, profit/loss statement, inventory, taxes and how to deal with the IRS. It's written in plain language anyone could understand and benefit from. For $1, the author sends an annual update of changes in the tax laws and other rates. Check your library or see the back of *Weaving Profits* to order this book.

Labor costs

After you have figured your indirect costs, the next amount to figure is the cost of your labor. This is the hourly wage you pay yourself, and if you hire employees, what you pay them. Add 30% of the hourly rate to cover social security and other payroll expenses.

For this example, say that you pay yourself $10 per hour. This is a good amount to use as a base. I found after the first six months in business that my own hourly rate never dipped below this.

For our purposes, say you have no employees. If you work only 40 hours a week (that'll be the day), 48 weeks a year (you'll need long vacations), the total number of hours worked in one year is 1,920. Multiply this times $10 and you get a total annual cost of labor as $19,200.

Cost of materials

Cost of materials is amount spent on yarns, accessories or any other materials to make an item. Don't include equipment which comes under indirect costs.

Let's use a handwoven rag rug as an example. Weight of the rags used comes to 3 pounds. Cost of the pre-cut rags was $1 per pound, giving you $3. You used 1/2 pound of warp yarn at $5 per pound plus .05 cents worth of sewing thread for finishing. Adding $3 + $2.50 + .05 gives a materials cost of $5.55 for one rug.

Now, double that amount. This is the necessary profit to collect on your materials to insure you make the same mark-up a retail outlet would charge a customer. Total materials cost is $11.10.

Production cost

We want to find out what it costs to produce one rag rug. Using the above amounts, we can figure the final production cost.

Add indirect costs, $9,960 to the labor costs for one year, $19,200 and you come up with $29,160. This is what it costs you to operate your business for a year. Divide $29,160 by the number of work hours, 1,920 to give an hourly cost of doing business of $15.19.

Be sure to double the cost of materials before passing on the charge to purchasers. Otherwise you're simply handing over the mark-up every retailer normally makes.

If one rug takes 2 hours to make, multiply $15.19 times 2 to give $30.38. Add in $11.10, the cost of materials to equal a total production cost of $41.48.

How to figure cost of yarns per piece

I use two ways to calculate the cost of yarn in each piece. If I use one fiber for the entire piece or one for warp and a different priced yarn for weft, I weigh the

29

woven fabric, including the cut-off ends, before washing and multiply the total number of ounces times the yarn price in ounces. With the warp and weft of different yarns, I estimate the warp yarn at 55% of the total weight and the weft at 45%.

When I use dissimilar priced yarns in warp and weft, which is much of the time, I list each yarn and how many yards there are to a pound. Say the warp width is 24" at 10 threads per inch and total warp length is 700". This warp contains six differently priced yarns. Out of 240 total warp threads, 40 threads come from an $8 per pound yarn at 1,500 yards per pound, 40 threads from a $16 per pound yarn at 1,000 yards per pound, and so on.

I multiply the number of threads of the $8 yarn times 700", which equals 28,000". Divide this by 36" (1 yard) giving 777.77 yards. Divide 777.77 yards by 1,500 yards to get .519 pound yarn. Multiply .519 times $8 gives $4.15 of the first yarn used.

Do this with the remainder of the warp threads and then the weft threads, being careful to measure your picks per inch. Though this process seems laborious, it goes quickly with a calculator. It gives a close dollar amount for yarn cost per piece.

Cost of sales

Now you have the cost of making one rug, but before you can set an accurate price, you need to know how much it costs you to sell the piece. Cost of sales is easy to figure. Say that you sold your rugs through 18 arts and crafts shows last year. You calculate that you spent an average of 30 hours per show, including driving, set-up, the hours of the show, tearing down and the drive home. Total hours spent to sell the rugs for the year were 540. If you sold a total of 360 rugs, divide 540 by the number of rugs, 360, to get an average time of 1.5 hours selling time per rug. At your hourly rate of $10 an hour, it cost you $15 to sell one rug.

It cost you $41.48 to make the piece and $15 to sell it, making your total expenses $56.48 per item. This amount is the floor price, or the least you can charge to insure a fair profit when selling at crafts shows or to other retail customers. Suppose you found from checking out your competition that similar rugs to yours are selling for between $75 and $100. You're hesitant, still, so you decide to set your price at $75, giving you a profit of $18.52 per piece.

If you set the retail price anywhere between $75 and $100, you are safely in line with what the market will bear. You also now know with confidence the exact amount of profit in each rug. If a customer wants to haggle over the price, you know how much you can afford to come down.

You can also test your prices from show to show and at different times of the year to see at what point the price affects sales. Typically, setting a higher price, within reason, will work to your advantage. This is because customers tend to assign higher value to more expensive items.

Setting wholesale prices

Pricing strategy is not much different for sales to wholesale accounts than at craft shows. For example, say you sold 400 rugs through stores or catalogs last year. You spent 20 hours making sales calls to get the accounts. Divide 20 hours by 400 rugs to get an average of three minutes to sell each rug. Multiply this times your hourly wage of $10 and you have an average cost of sales of .50 per item. Add this .50 to the production cost of $41.48. This equals a wholesale floor price of $41.98.

Stores normally double the price of what they buy. This is known as 'keystoning'. Your accounts pay you $41.98 for one rug and sell it for $94. You can see how different the profit margin is for sales in the two different settings. There was more profit in the rugs sold at crafts shows, but less time and effort spent selling wholesale.

Item profitability

Doing an item profitability chart for each of your products shows at a glance which item brings the most profit in a given market. This gives you a total picture of where you make the most money. You can use this information to decide what to weave, how much to weave and where to sell. See the example of the rag rug's profitability in Figure 2.2 following. Besides doing a profit chart, you'll want to keep an inventory record of sales for every item. Chapters 10 and 11 explain how to use inventory systems and set priorities for more profitable products.

An example inventory chart in Figure 2.3, on page 33, shows you the volume of sales for each market. It lists sales by the month, quarter or year. Here you can see that catalog sales of the rag rug were slow in September, but craft shows and store sales were okay. Looking at the profitability chart fig 2.2, you see that sales through catalogs are losing money. This suggests dropping the catalog market and doing more craft shows, or opening more store accounts, where cost of sales is low.

These tables will help you set criteria for making more profitable decisions based on your personal selling experiences. You can make your own charts like these or modify them to suit your needs.

What happens when you find through your calculations that a product is loosing money? You can try to cut the costs of producing it. Try making longer warps that saves on the threading and sleying time. Or you can use lower cost yarns. See Chapter 9 for production saving tips. You might find, however, it would be better to drop the item completely and focus on more profitable pieces.

One-of-a-kind pieces

If a piece is one-of-a-kind or part of a limited edition series, setting the price must account for the intrinsic value in addition to the information in the formulas above. How do you put a price on your art? If you are new at the business, try to find similar pieces by several other artisans and stay in that

Figure 2.2 Item profit worksheet

Item: Rag rug				
Market	Sales amount	Production cost	Cost of sales	Profit
Craft shows	75.00	41.48	15.00	18.52
Home shows	75.00	41.48	7.00	26.52
Stores	45.00	41.48	.50	3.02
Reps	45.00	41.48	21.50	-17.98
Catalog	49.00	41.48	18.50	-10.98
Other				

DROP THESE MARKETS

range. By the time you become famous, your work will have found its price level. In a free market system, the dollar value of art seems to do that on its own.

You can get by for a long time with guesswork about how you're doing with pricing your work, but if you wonder why you have plenty of sales but still aren't making money, chances are good you need to do the kind of analysis we have looked at here.

Figure 2.3 Inventory of items' sales by market

Total sales of items by markets in:
Month: Sept.   Quarter: III   Year: 1991

Market	Rag rugs	Pillows	Throws	Placemats	Wall Hangings	Total
Shows	12	2	4	8	1	27
Boutiques						
Stores	8	1	7			16
Direct mail				4		4
Catalog	1			4	2	7
Reps						
Total	21	3	11	16	3	

Chapter 3   Easy First Sales

Selling to friends, neighbors and relatives

The easiest way to start selling is simply to start producing. When your friends and relatives see the products you make, they'll want them. You may have experienced some of these easy sales already. When I sent some of my first handwoven garments as gifts to my sister and mother, the pieces were so admired by their friends, they set up a home party for me to show at. These early sales at friendly events boosted my confidence.

Door-to-door sales

You're probably thinking door-to-door selling may be OK for encyclopedias and vacuum cleaners, but handwovens? I heard a story of someone who did quite well with this method. I was showing my work at a craft show in Albuquerque, when an older gentleman approached my booth. Seeing me with my work, reminded him of his own weaving experience. He was interested in weaving from an early age because his mother had been a weaver. She taught him and his children, her grandchildren, how to weave rag rugs and encouraged them to sell the pieces in the neighborhood. They went door-to-door taking orders from a variety of samples and a price list. Sales were consistent and the money was good. They did the weaving and the selling after school and made their own spending money from the business.

There's no reason this form of business could not work well for you with items for the home like rugs, placemats, pillows, throws and bedspreads. The only cost of making the sales is your time and effort. The cost of materials for making rag rugs and placemats comes to less expense per piece than almost any other handwoven products. I found thrift stores willing to sell huge bags of clothing unsuitable for resale for only a few dollars. There are also several companies that sell rag material pre-cut in one or two inch widths on tubes that would save you cutting the rags yourself. When I was living in New York City, I would often see rolls of these cut-off fabrics on tubes laying outside sewing warehouses in garbage heaps.

You could also sell woven jewelry door to door as well, but if you offer home products first, you can later expand your lines to sell to customers who know and trust you. Weave a set of samples of everything you make, print up an order form and price list of custom sizes, and then go out and take orders.

This is a perfect starting place for a part-time or full-time business. The only obstacle for most is the knocking on doors. You must be the kind of individual who isn't discouraged by having the door slam shut on you at any time. The great thing is, it doesn't cost anything to try. This is also a way of building a base of customers who might later want to sponsor home parties.

Home parties (boutiques)

A home party is a great starting place for selling your craft. A friend that's seen and bought your work will often be flattered to host an evening or afternoon party, especially if you offer a commission of 10 to 15% of the sales. Most of the time, they want to take weaving instead of cash.

The best times for these events is between 7 and 10 PM. Invite as many persons as your host is comfortable with. Call everyone that you think might have an interest in your work and encourage them to bring their friends.

Put some refreshments out and have a party. At some point, you could give a brief talk or demonstration about your weaving, maybe on a small portable or inkle loom. The more you know and can talk about your weaving, the more value the listeners will put on the products. It's easy to get excited about something you make with your own hands. You can feel when this enthusiasm transfers to the listener.

Make it clear that payment should be made at the time. Once someone has paid for something, they are less inclined to change their mind about it later. Acquaintances may take familiarity as an invitation to open a charge account with you. Unless you want to deal with the hassles of accounts payable, require payment with the sale.

Because it costs little produce a show like this, you might discount your normal prices as an incentive for persons to come. Also, announce that anyone being a host to a party for you will receive a commission. I found, though, my sponsors usually wanted to take their percentage in woven products. This is great, because you have less to pay out.

If you like these events, you could expand into larger productions. You might, through your home party contacts, seek sponsoring by a local organization in return for a commission on the sales. You could invite a few other craftspersons to show their work and charge a fee or percentage of their sales. You wouldn't want competing products. But maybe you have a friend with a complementary line. For example you weave clothing, another craftsperson makes handbags or wall hangings. Maybe a jeweler and a potter would fit in, too.

These events could become popular enough that you would have to find a larger place and rent selling spaces to more vendors. This could grow into its own business after awhile and you might find yourself spending more time organizing shows than weaving. See Chapter 15, for more on becoming a show producer.

Co-ops

If you like working with partners, consider joining a cooperative gallery with other craftspersons. Co-ops require little investment from you and provide an excellent way to test your products and display ideas. There are many operations like this across the country. Most of them have a jurying process similar to the arts and crafts shows. Call or visit one to find out how they interview new artists.

Each co-op gallery will have its own rules of operating. In some, you will be required to work at the gallery some hours per month and pay monthly dues. Others charge a monthly rental fee and hire sales help and bookkeepers to operate the business. You may or may not have to pay a commission of the retail sales to the gallery.

Some of my best sales have come through galleries that were jointly owned by several artists. Usually their involvement in the gallery is a means to promote their own work, so their support for you as an artisan will be more helpful. There are advantages for everyone involved; fewer hours to work per partner, higher percentage of the retail price going to the artist/owner, and access to greater media exposure from being a gallery owner.

The above ideas for selling your work are the least costly to you in expense. This is because they require more effort in time and personal contacts. If this way of selling seems *too* personal or threatening, try arts and crafts shows. Here, the public comes to you and often buy on impulse, with minimum effort from you.

Chapter 4 Craft Shows: Hidden Treasures Lure Thousands

Though today's craft fairs are looked on as a source of handcrafted novelties and collectibles, the outdoor market is probably the oldest historical business tradition known. People made their crafts and foods and brought them to the marketplace to sell or trade. Even now in other countries around the world, the common market is a part of the majority of the people's everyday reality. We in the U.S. of course have our own tradition known as the Mall.

I never go to a mall if I can help it; when I do, I'm always struck by how the public seems obsessed with shopping. People love to shop. Some of them even like to buy, but what they enjoy most is the lively activity of a market-place.

This excitement over shopping is even more present in the arts and crafts shows. When you wander around a craft fair today, you can sense an excitement from artisans selling their exotic hand made wares and seekers hunting treasures for a bargain.

Advantages of craft shows

A craft show is a good starting point for selling your work. Beyond the dates of the show, there are no commitments. You can do one or two and walk away, with a minimum of expense of your time and money and probably a fatter wallet. Or, you might decide you like what happens and take up the crafts fair life-style and make it the mainstay of your business.

In a crafts fair, you have your own scaled down model of a retail store, even if it's only for two or three days. You can use a show to test new products, designs, price changes and booth displays. You are directly in touch with the marketplace, so if you're work isn't selling, you will find out why from customers' reactions.

In selling direct to the public, you will keep the entire amount of the sales, minus expenses. When the show is over, it's over. Since most shows are held on weekends, you have your week free to create more pieces. You have control of your time. It's a great feeling to go to a movie in the middle of the week when everyone else is laboring under canned air, moronic bosses and minimum wages.

Awards

Many better craft shows offer prizes or cash awards for best display or best designer. One friend I worked with to help start her business won first prize in fiber arts at the *Dallas 500* show in Texas at her second or third show.

Getting recognition isn't just strokes for the ego, it adds considerable value to your work in the eyes of customers. It also affords you speaking and teaching opportunities as a recognized professional, another avenue for building demand of your work. More publicity and recognition equals higher perceived value by your customers. Besides the publicity value, award winners often receive prize money. Most state fairs have juried events with large cash awards.

Prestige you get from such awards will almost guarantee you feature articles in your local periodicals and newspapers. There is more on how to make use of this kind of free publicity in Chapters 7 and 8.

How to apply

Applications for shows will be mailed upon request from the show producers. Once you are on their mailing list you will probably continue to receive applications for a few years. Most applications are due three to six months before the actual show date. Some larger events like the ACE (American Craft Enterprises) shows, may require jurying a year or more in advance.

Better shows are juried. This means that the artist must submit slides or photos of their recent work and possibly a photo of their booth display to the show producer, along with a jury fee.

Many craftspersons agree that jury fees are unfair. A well known craft show may receive more than 800 applications for as few as 200 booth spaces. If each applicant sends in a $15 jury fee, the show promoters receive $12,000 dollars before they even collect the booth rental fees. I have resolved to look on the expense as just another cost of doing business. If you want to get into the better shows, you have to play by their rules.

In a home party, no one will mind if you are putting on the venture with someone else. Craft shows can be a different matter. If you read the rules included with the application blanks for most shows, you will often see a requirement that artists sharing booths pay an additional fee. Personally, I think this is unfair. If I invite another weaver to help and bring some of her work, I simply apply for the show in my name and put my friend's work out with mine. I don't recommend doing this at the larger ACC shows or whole-sale trade shows, unless you form a company with the other weavers. Confusion that results when a store buyer wants one weaver's work over the other's could result in harsh feelings and possible financial altercations. Besides, some shows are too good for sales to risk violations that might bar you from future admission. Nevertheless, no show management will mind if you have helpers.

When two people split the rent for a space at a crafts fair, it is easier on each one's pocketbook. Not only are these cooperative ventures economically sound, they generate more enthusiasm and pleasure for everyone. Of course, you must get along with your partners.

How to better your chances of getting in

There is no guarantee that you will be accepted into a show with your first application. Shows you do once, will often give you preference for reentry. Increase your chances of acceptance by following these guidelines:

1) Slides are often *THE* chief component in your acceptance by a jury. With hundreds of applicants, it is the quality of your photos or slides that secures you entry into a show. So, you may have to spend extra money to get top-notch pictures of your best work.

Count on making several sets of slides of 6 to 12 different pieces, plus your booth display. Often, you will send off one set to apply for a show and need another set for other applications also due. Some shows do not return the slides until the event.

2) If you're required to submit actual samples of your work, be sure to send your most detailed pieces. Technical execution may outshine design elements. If a display is needed, assemble it at home first to make sure it is sturdy and does not distract a viewer from the work itself.

3) Follow instructions in the application form, word for word. Fill the information in completely, either by printing clearly or typing. Slides should be labeled in accord with their guidelines. Protect slides in envelope protectors made for sending slides. Enclose your application, photos or slides, jury fee, if any, and a SASE. If you don't follow their directions, they won't consider your application.

4) Apply early. Sometimes it's first come, first serve.

5) Many juries look for consistency of style among pieces. This shows your concentration on developing artistic excellence within a medium or theme. They aren't looking for pretty models or beautiful backgrounds.

6) If you apply to the American Craft Enterprise shows, they will send you information on how to make better slides of your work. Since their shows are some of the best in the country, it would be worth your time to apply. Write to American Craft Enterprises, PO Box 10, New Paltz, NY 12561, (800) 527-3844, or (914) 883-6100.

Last minute cancellations

Here's a tip for the brave and adventurous. Almost every show I have attended has had last minute cancellations or no-shows by exhibitors. Can you guess how easy it is to get a space early in the opening hours of the show? Few promoters will refuse to take your money to fill the space. Nevertheless, they will probably want cash up front, so be ready.

To get into shows this way you should come prepared to set up your booth at the last minute of set-up time before the show opens to the public. You should take a good look at the space, however, before you hand over your money. If the spot is on the end of a long string of booths, sales can be too poor to pay your expenses.

I have heard of at least one craftsperson who never sends in applications for shows, but always uses the above method. I was able to get into two major selling shows, at the last minute, that I'd been unable to get into through the normal application procedure.

Choosing the right show

Do your first shows close to home, within one hundred miles. There are two good reasons; lower gas and mileage, and less stress. A shorter drive and a longer night's sleep give you more energy for the show.

Shows can be both exciting and demanding. Hundreds, possibly thousands, of potential customers come by your booth, many of whom will look at your work and talk to you briefly. It helps if a friend or spouse can assist you. Setting up the booth and handling sales goes more easily with two persons, but be careful not to impede the flow of traffic into your selling space. At some point, you will want to take a break, or walk around and see the other booths; this you can't do unless you have a partner.

Which shows should you apply to? Visit a show beforehand to see if it's for you. If you can't go yourself, ask a friend that lives nearby to go. If that's not possible you'll have to rely on asking other craftspersons and information in the craft show guides. Show guides are mentioned later in this chapter. Talking to other craftspeople, however, may or may not give you a good perspective on whether your work would sell well at particular events, but if several exhibitors tell you a show is good, then you're probably safe.

Of course, some events are better than others. Large craft shows with hundreds of exhibitors that ACC puts on five times a year, average sales per booth from $4,000 to $20,000. Many craftspeople try to get into these shows, so competition is intense. Once you get in the first year, however, it's not as hard to get accepted again. If you can get into these shows early in your career, you may find yourself selling your work a lot more quickly than you can make it.

Types of craft shows

When selecting shows, choose the kind of event that will attract buyers of the products you make. Shows can be divided into three types with some shows mixing these entries. One is fine arts, only. At fine art shows, you will find paintings, photos, sculpture and other media often seen in galleries. Two is art and craft shows where you see many different craft forms and art or art reproductions. Three is country craft shows.

Country craft shows are distinctly different from the more highly juried art and craft shows, though you may not be able to tell this from some of the show guide reviews. To present the image of a high quality show, the promoters claim that entries into these shows are juried. Their main criteria for entry is that you aren't selling assembled kits or imported products. You should see one just to know what they are about. The crafts exhibited are all similar, most of them easily produced, and selling from $2 to $50. These shows might work well for handwoven placemats or other small gift items. I have tried them with high-end woven clothing and did not do well. When selling higher priced items, choose the more established, competitive juried arts and crafts shows.

Other kinds of shows

Renaissance fairs

Another type of art and craft show that needs special mention is the renaissance fair. These outdoor events include craft booths as a part of a total entertainment package. All the vendors dress in medieval costume and booths have the same theme. A variety of food, drink, jugglers, jousters, knights and fair maidens abound at these festivals. Most renaissance shows run every weekend from one to two months. In your contract, you're required to do most weekends of the show.

You are responsible for building a substantial booth in the medieval theme. It must be sturdier than normal craft shows because it will be up for several weeks. Count on spending $1,000 to $2,000 to build a good booth. Since you rent the space for most of the weeks of the show, you become a lessee or tenant.

Management also takes a percentage of your sales. Even with that, it pays off for some. Many craftspersons do so well at these shows they only do renaissance shows. They become 'permanent' fixtures for several years.

Mall shows

In most craft show guides, you will find listings for shows held in shopping malls. Mall shows are produced by the mall management, a show promoter or a local organization. These shows are usually part of a tour sponsored by a producer putting on events in one or several nearby states. Many exhibitors follow the circuit for several weeks, especially in the fall and pre-Christmas months.

At mall shows, you see more fine arts than you see crafts. Many shopping centers have restrictions on what can be sold; they don't want you to compete with their stores. I have been denied entry in some shows because I sold clothing. In one way, I was lucky. Few of these shows do well for high end crafts. If you make smaller items in the $10 to $50 price range, you might do okay. Even though rental fees are cheaper, sales are often lower than amounts you would receive from craft shows. Promoters usually ask a small space fee, plus a percentage of the sales.

You can always find a good selling crafts show with far better attendance than a mall show. When you can't, they remain an option for otherwise empty weekends. Mall shows might help, too, in slow months like January and February.

One year, I decided to try a mall show in January with a promoter who did several malls in the Southwest. Her shows had received good reviews in *Sunshine Artists,* a magazine listing a show calendar and reviews by craftspersons doing shows around the country. (See the Appendix). This show was held in a busy shopping mall in Albuquerque. I thought I would try it for the experience of something different and because there weren't any good craft shows nearby at that time of year.

This show went for four days, beginning at 10:00 A.M. and going till 9:00 P.M.. By accident, I had a large space, much bigger than spaces at any crafts show I had ever done, perhaps 25' by 25'. The promoter encouraged me to bring a loom and weave during the show. Most of the customers walking by who saw me weaving, stopped to look or ask questions. This often generated a crowd. Though I spent more time talking than I did weaving, I made several sales and received a few special orders as a result of demonstrating.

Total retail sales from the show were about $1,300. I picked up one whole-sale account with an initial order of $500. Also, I was able to weave about $500 worth of inventory at retail prices during the four days. My cost of doing the show came to about $150, and the location was close enough that I could drive home every night.

I decided to do the following week in another mall, with the same promoter, in another city. Sales were about $500 lower, and the one lead I got to a wholesale account didn't work out. It turned into a long exhausting two weeks, but it was worth it, considering how dead January and February usually are.

The promoter of the shows above, told me a story about some other weavers she had met. Exhibiting at several of her mall shows in Texas, a wife/husband weaving team set up two small portable looms back-to-back and wove placemats. They piled the woven mats on tables near the looms. This was their whole set-up. Their prices were inexpensive and the products did not compete with stores in the mall. But the real beauty of the situation was, they could produce their inventory while they were selling. During the weeks right before Christmas, they couldn't weave fast enough to keep up with sales. Sounds good to me.

It's easy to overlook alternative markets for handwoven fabrics that might be quite lucrative. Yet it can be much easier to fill a niche market than trying to produce several different types of products. You can find out about shows for any type of business or interest group by looking in magazines devoted to the subject. Your library will have a copy of the *Standard Periodical*

Directory by Oxbridge, which lists magazines and journals by subject index. For other sources of special interest group shows, see Chapter 6, Wholesale Trade Shows. Events for special interest markets for your handwovens or other craft products include, but aren't limited to:

Local fashion shows. Local women's social groups produce fashion shows for original work. Call your chamber of commerce and check the library for listings of associations in your area. Also visit the large hotels and convention centers and speak with their public relations person. They have schedules of upcoming shows and lists of producers to get in touch with.

Horse shows. What would you sell to horses? Many thoroughbreds purchase handwoven saddleblankets for their owners. At least, most owners think their horses are smart enough to do this. If you have ever been around persons who love horses, you know what an enthusiastic group they are. They love to spend money for fancy saddleblankets and equipment. Many horse shows sell booth space to vendors. One weaver I know of, exhibits only at horse shows. Big events draw the largest crowds, like the Kentucky Derby. The Arabian Horse Show and others travel from city to city. *Standard Periodical Directory* lists scores of horse and rider magazines for finding information on these events.

Home shows and boat shows. Most major cities have a home show and a boat show at least once a year. Here you could sell rugs, pillows, tapestry screens and other items used in interiors. See Chapter 8.

Jewelry shows. Sometimes you see large jewelry shows in convention centers once or more a year. Though most of the jewelry is silver or gold, handwoven earrings, bracelets and necklaces might do well because of the hand-made attraction.

Antique shows. Antique furnishings are often in need of upholstering. What could add as much value to an heirloom as handwoven fabric? Antique automobiles could be reupholstered in unique fabric from your loom, too.

Craft show guides

There are several resources that list craft shows around the country and give information about show performance in previous years. If you buy these guides, and you should, get the most current issues available. Show performance changes over the years due to causes you have no other way of knowing about. Some shows simply fold up and disappear. Compare different reviews for the same show. If the reports are similar among various guides, then you can consider them good bets.

The Appendix lists several major guides. They may seem expensive, but I have often made back, or saved, more than the cost of these books by selecting or avoiding a show because of what I learned from them. Weeding out the bad shows is worth the price alone.

Announcements of show events can be found in periodicals like *Sunshine Artists, The Crafts Report, Handwoven, Fiberarts,* and *Shuttle Spindle & Dyepot. Sunshine Artists* gives reviews every month on shows in states where they have craftspersons reporting. *The Crafts Report* gives sales and attendance figures of the bigger craft and wholesale shows. For instance, the Philadelphia Craft Show held in November, 1991 projected total retail sales of over $2 million. Average sales for wearable fiber exhibitors was around $14,000 each and non-wearable fibers averaged around $9,500 each. Pretty good, yeah?

Another source of art and craft shows will be your state arts council. They should be listed in the government pages of your phone book. If not, write the National Assembly of State Arts Agencies, 1010 Vermont Ave. NW, Suite 920, Washington, DC 20005 for information on your state.

Before you apply to a show, visit it yourself, find out what the show guides say about it, and talk to other craftspersons who have done the event. Here's what you need to find out.

- How many booth spaces are being rented for the whole show? A show with 500 booths will draw bigger crowds than one with only 50.

- Is the show outdoors or inside? Has weather affected previous attendance?

- Is the show well known? Does the promoter advertise in the newspapers, on radio, billboards or TV? Better shows are successfully promoted as annual events. The public knows about them and returns faithfully every year to see what's new.

- What are the security arrangements? Most outdoor events have no effective way of guarding your merchandise. Unless you secure your booth from possible entry, you should count on packing up and taking your goods at the end of each day of the show. Indoor shows are safer in this regard. The building is locked at a given time and often, there will be an overnight guard.

● Do other weavers exhibit? Does their work sell? Don't expect them all to tell you, though some might. If there aren't any other weavers, there may not be enough product recognition by the public attending the show. This means the crowd simply doesn't know what they're looking at. I once did a show in Dallas produced by Biggest Little Craft Shows Ever. I picked the show because it got good reviews in the Sunshine Artists Audit book mentioned later, and I had relatives I could stay with, and it was on the way to Houston, where I had two larger shows lined up. At the time, I knew nothing about 'country craft' shows, which this one was. I took in about $450 in sales for $270 in expenses. I was the only weaver showing; I no longer wonder why. The worst of it was comments like *"how come your ponchos are $150 and they're only $20 at K-Mart.?"* There was definitely a lack of product recognition here.

● Flea markets attract the kind of buyers that want fifty cent bargains. They are a waste of your time and money for selling handwovens or other fine crafts, though they're a great place to shop for fixtures and booth covers.

Planning your show schedule

Shows in the three or four months before Christmas will *usually* produce higher sales than at other times. Some organizations hold craft events in the spring and again in the fall. The fall shows are often better. No matter when you start your business, budget enough money for shows in the pre-Christmas months as your highest priority. Plan your production so that you will have plenty of inventory on hand.

If you like doing shows and decide to travel more than a day's drive to get there, it makes sense to line up events en route, signing up for two or three shows, back-to-back in nearby areas. Some craftspeople produce their whole inventory in several months and then follow a circuit of shows, selling every weekend for the few months before Christmas. A cautionary note; doing several shows in a row can be exhausting. Even one show can knock you out for a day or two. Until you know what you can comfortably endure, be conservative with how many you sign up to do.

If you plan to sell your work to stores too, use the time between weekends of shows to visit shops where you are traveling. Store owners will give you feedback on your woven products for different geographical areas.

It happens frequently that two different shows you want to be in are scheduled for the same weekend. Unless you have a guaranteed spot in one of them, apply for both and wait to see which one accepts you. You're cost will be the two jury fees, but at least you're covered if one rejects your application.

Consider doing shows in cities where you have friends or relatives. If you have a place to stay free, why pay $30 a night for a motel? Of course, they might have kids, dogs, and lots of energy to talk. There's something to be said for the quiet of a motel. Staying with relatives and friends can be supportive, or a source of tension.

You can find decent motel rooms for between $20 and $25 a night. It requires some checking when you pull into town, so count on extra time for research. It's easier to find vacancies in the afternoon than it is after dark. You can find lower cost motels on the outskirts of towns on truck routes or old state highways. Once you find a good motel, keep their business card for future trips. It's a great relief to know you have a comfortable room ahead of you after hours of driving or doing a show.

For easier planning, get a big map of the United States and a large wall calendar with all the months of the year on one page. Use the calendar to show dates and deadlines for applications. By referring to the road map, you can plot travel time and rest stops in advance. Also collect maps of cities and states you travel through. Your first time in a new town is the hardest. Next year, you'll know where to stay and how to get around the area.

High booth fees do not always guarantee the show will be a good selling one, though most of the better shows are more costly. Several promoters, like Harvest Festival and Steve Powers Shows, put on circuits of scheduled events each weekend for several months running. Booth rentals are high, but they do extensive advertising, provide entertainment, and pull in good crowds. They prefer craftspeople to do several of the shows on the tour, but some allow you to try one to test your sales.

One of these shows in Houston yielded the biggest weekend sales I ever had, but the next year and the following year sales kept dropping and fewer craftspeople exhibited. Even the promoters felt the show wasn't happening anymore, so they dropped the show. Stay on top of information on these changes by making friends with other craftspeople. The crafts grapevine is alive with good news and bad news about what's happening with different events and geographic locations.

Avoid first-time shows

I have to stress this, **AVOID FIRST-TIME SHOWS!** I had heard this advice repeatedly and always followed the obvious logic. Most craft shows are annual events that the public has attended for several years. How can a new show expect to draw good crowds?

One day, I slipped. A promoter called from a state where I had done a show two years before. He had 'great news' about their first venture into Albuquerque, 50 miles from me. Because I had exhibited with them before, I had first choice on a location. He offered me an extra booth space if I brought my loom and demonstrated. He also told me they were doing extensive radio, TV, billboards and newspaper ads. So, I signed up for a double corner booth in the middle of the exhibit hall.

It cost me $200 to do the show. I sold nothing the entire three days. This was a first for me. It was also, unequivocally, the last time I will ever do a first-timer. The worst part about this show, the final insult, and ultimate degradation was being subjected to a constant barrage of persons coming by the booth trying to sell me something, including 2 charities, one flower girl, 3 candy hawkers disguised as boy scouts, 3 new co-op store owners and 4 promoters trying to fill booth space in *their* new shows. Their favorite line was *"We're almost filled now, but I think I can find you a space . . ."* Sure, I'll bet you can.

Because there are so many good shows around, it seems as if everyone wants to get into the act. There has been a great proliferation of self styled promoters aiming to get rich off show rental fees from craftspeople. These person's prime interest is to make a buck off you. Don't be misled by their hard sell tactics about getting in on the ground floor NOW! . . . while there's still space left.

No matter how carefully you have chosen and prepared for a show, you sometimes run into some real dogs. I still hear some of mine barking from way back. All you can do is think of it as a continuing education.

Booth location

In good shows it doesn't matter where you set up, you're going to sell, but typically, booth spaces on a corner, near the center, entrance or exit of a show are better selling spots than spaces on the aisles. Avoid getting near the food vendors or entertainment. Food is the number one seller at shows and not only are you competing for attention, you must deal with junk food being carried in and around your pieces. Noise from loud music will prevent you from being able to talk to your customers pleasantly.

Request booth locations with your application if you know where you want to be. I've had requests acknowledged often, despite the application stating otherwise. If you have done a show in the past, managers may give you the same location or at least, give your booth preference a higher priority.

Last minute cancellations leave empty spaces. If your allotted space is unacceptable, ask the show manager if you can trade in the first hours of setting up. You won't be the only one looking to switch, so get there quick with your request. Most shows are run by nice folks. All they can do is say no.

Craft show booths aren't large. Most shows give you a single 10' wide by 10' long. Unless you are splitting the expenses with another weaver or craftsperson with complementary products, it is unusual to get enough sales to justify renting two booths. Double the space means double the rent. Be sure when you are applying for the show, what the exact booth size will be. Make your display flexible enough to fit in a smaller 8'x 8' space, if that's all you will get.

How to display your products

Once you are accepted, design your booth to show your work in a neat, orderly arrangement. It should be easy and inviting for the customer to walk in and touch the merchandise. Yes, that's right, you want them to touch the pieces. Woven items are attractive because of the way they feel. Allow the product to help sell itself. If a product is too delicate to be handled, it may not do well in the craft show market.

The fuller your display, the more you will sell, no matter what the product. Customers buy more from a full rack or table. If they see gaps, dishevelled garments or a scattered pile of items, they feel the work is picked over too much. Keep your racks and tables neat the whole time of the show. It may mean going over to straighten merchandise many times during the day, but the customer should feel they are the first ones to see your work. Also, items displayed closest to the customer will be the easiest to sell. Place your most attractive pieces in the front of your fixtures or racks.

Use tables and hanging dowels for displaying blankets or throws, placemats, rugs and other flat items. They can be arranged in neat clean stacks on the tables or in a waterfall descent from a standing display rack. Rugs look great this way. Customers can see some portion of every piece. Look at a carpet or rug store for ideas on how to show large flat woven work. This is a good way to learn how to display any item. Follow the examples of retailers who are succeeding in selling products to the public.

Also, visit craft shows and see how other craftspersons display their work. You'll change your display as you do more shows. Experiences will teach you what works well and what doesn't. By my second year, I had changed my display at least three times.

It is important that the booth make the customer feel free to enter and browse through the merchandise. Build your display at home first, and play with variations of how the arrangement looks with your pieces displayed. You will have better success by carrying related products in your booth. For example, display all clothing related items, or have a booth that sells rag rugs, pillows and throws, or concentrate on woven jewelry work. Too many products together look junky and distracting.

Arrange merchandise in product groups, then put similar colors together. Customers are used to shopping in stores where they can always see and find the colors they want. Offer a wide array of colors. A large selection will make some colors sell better than others. Customers like variety.

Experiment for a few shows with your arrangement and see how the public acts toward it. If you notice frequent hesitation or turning away from your display, try altering the arrangement to make it more inviting.

Make sure every item has a label and a hanging tag with the price and your name and address. Don't put the price on the label, though, because many of your sales will be given as gifts. Some customers have the feeling of being cheated if they have to ask for the price of something. They wonder too, if the person that comes along after them will hear the same amount.

If you have to divert your attention to answer one customer's question about price, another browser has an opportunity to walk away. Avoid this kind of loss by pricing and labeling everything in advance. Be ready to conclude a sales transaction quickly.

If you sell clothing or woven jewelry, have a mirror and a dressing room. Customers can then see how the piece looks on them. This is important. Get the person to try a piece on and the sale is halfway made.

Fixtures

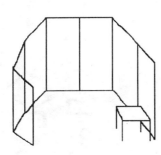

Fixtures, racks, grids and tables can be used to hang or place your products on. Metal or chrome fixtures sell merchandise better than wood displays.

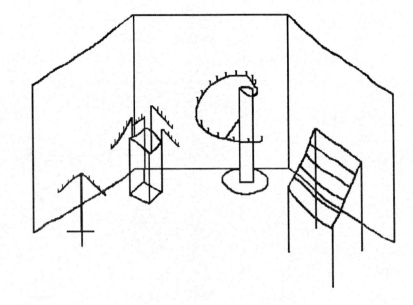

Wood racks are more attractive and natural, but they also look more expensive. There is a subtle message conveyed to the customer that your fixtures are expensive, so your product must be, too.

What is more important, the public is conditioned to shopping in stores with metallic fixtures. In every store carrying apparel, you will see clothing displayed on waterfall or descending spiral fixtures; all chrome, all shiny. By imitating the big retail experts, you can sell more to customers that are trained to buy from these kinds of displays. Take advantage of a consumer habit already in motion.

You can find used fixtures cheaply from stores going out of business. Watch your local newspaper classifieds. Some have a 'Fixtures' sub-heading. Many cities have used fixture stores where you can buy or rent at prices cheaper than you can buy new pieces. There are also fixture catalogs that you can order items by mail. Look for their ads in the craft magazines listed in the appendix. Also, check the library for books listing catalogs, like those listed on page 88 in Chapter 7.

On the other hand, some craftspersons use wood to build a display themselves. At craft shows, you see many booths that are custom made. If you choose to use wood, you can make fixtures yourself or with help from a woodworking friend. Be sure they can withstand the pressures of wind and constant customer handling. Also, they should be light enough that you can load and unload them from your car by yourself.

Booth cover

For protection against the sun and unexpected changes in the weather, acquire a canopy or covering that will adequately protect you and your pieces. You only need to get rained on once to realize how important this is. Use a frame and cover that is sturdy enough to withstand high winds, rain and large crowds. White tarps or cover material work best, as colored tarps will cause the light to be tinted and affect the appearance of your merchandise.

You want adventure, danger and suspense from a good movie, not from your booth covering. You could easily face a lawsuit, if your homemade frame blows down onto a customer's child or the potter next to you. At best, you'll find yourself the owner of a large collection of pottery shards. Physical safety of your customers, fellow craftspersons, and your own merchandise should be a priority in constructing your booth.

If you have a friend with tools and some construction skills, you can design a structure to suit your own needs. But unless you are confident about your skills, save yourself the trouble by investing in a well known brand cover like the KD canopy. There are booth suppliers that sell displays ready to set up and designed for the craftsperson doing outdoor shows. A list of these companies is in the appendix. Most of them run ads in periodicals like *The Crafts Report.*

You sometimes come across other craftspeople selling their fixtures or displays, either because they are buying better set-ups, or because they're not doing outdoor shows anymore. Other sources are flea markets and the yellow pages under 'Tents and Awnings'.

Customer mailing list

Create a mailing list of your customers' names and addresses. Whenever someone makes a purchase or inquiry, enter their name on the list. When you return to the same city to do another show, drop them a postcard with details of the show's date, and if you know it, your booth location. Your weaving is regarded as 'collectible'. You will find regular customers collecting your new pieces every year.

I've had customers come to a show just to see my recent work and make another purchase. If you let your customers know when and where you will be, most of them will come by; if for no reason except to say hi, and how much they enjoy the piece they bought from you. This is a great opportunity for you to show your latest creations.

Accepting credit cards

Credit card purchases can increase your sales by 30% to 40%. This is especially true for high ticket items at craft shows where the purchaser may not have enough cash.

As a credit card merchant, you pay a discount fee to the bank processing the transaction (usually 3% to 8%) on each sale. Recently my bank added a monthly minimum service charge of $15, applied against discounts of sales.

This means, if I have no credit card sales in a given month, I still pay a $15 fee.

Merchants are required to call an 800 number for authorization when the sales amount is over a 'floor limit', usually $50, sometimes $75. This means sales under that amount do not require telephone approval. Also, every week you receive a small booklet with list of lost, stolen or invalid card numbers. You can quickly check card numbers against this list before you conclude the transaction.

Unless you are located near a pay phone and you have a friend who can watch the booth while you make the call, it's impractical to try to call in on every large purchase. My daring solution is to wait until the show is over to make the authorization calls. The customer already has the piece, so if the credit card service says no, I'm stuck. Yet, I've never had a card that did not pass authorization, though a friend of mine did. She got stuck with a loss of about $150.

There are rules you must observe to maintain your merchant status. You are not allowed to deposit other merchant's sales. You cannot split large tickets into two smaller ones to avoid the floor limit check. Banks will give you a full list of the regulations. If you violate the bank's policies, they will close your account and it will be extremely difficult to renew your standing.

To get merchant status, apply to a bank for a merchant account, most can accept credit card deposits. When you approach banks, be aware of the following:

- Banks get a discount fee of 3% to 8% of the total for each sale. Discount rates that the bank charges you, vary from bank to bank. You can find out the various rates by calling the banks and asking what their credit card discount rates are for merchant accounts. They will want to know your average sales price per item and your average sales per year. Higher priced sales such as $150 might allow you a lower discount, but every bank has different rates and policies.

- There is a set-up fee to get started; usually around $30 for the credit card machine and another $30 for supplies of sales and deposit tickets. In addition, some banks charge a service charge on a monthly basis, if your sales do not reach a certain amount. A typical charge is $15 per month. Banks don't like to give credit card accounts to mail order businesses or other types of business with high incidences or likelihood of fraud.

- Merchants must have a physical business location, usually in the same county as the bank. They look for a street address, not a P.O. box. Set up your studio as a shop and make sales from there. This way if the bank wants to see a physical location, you can provide them with one. Put up some displays of your work and make it look like a retail outlet. And while you are at it, why not make it a real store?

- Banks prefer to work with their known customers. You should have been operating with a business checking account for at least one year.

- You need a business license, sales tax permit, a federal tax ID number and other documents that prove you are a legitimate business.

Organizations that will help you locate banks granting credit card merchant status are American Craft Retailers Ass'n, Box 9, Woodstock, MD 21163, and American Craft Ass'n, 21 S. Eltings Corner Rd., Highland, NY 12528.

My first year in business, I didn't accept credit cards. I thought it would be too difficult to get an account. Many of the other craftspersons around me at the shows were taking cards, so I realized I was probably losing sales. Lots of cards were passing through those little credit card machines. As it turned out, it was easy to get the account. I chose a bank that was actively seeking new business accounts and was less strict about inspecting the physical location of my business. When I started accepting credit cards, my sales picked up by 30%.

Accepting checks

As easy as credit cards might be for the customer, they cost you a percentage of the sale when they are used. You might do better to ask for a check. Tell customers you would prefer to take their check instead of their credit card, but if they say no, don't push it. Taking checks has these advantages:

- You can easily record their name and address for your mailing list.

- You don't have to pay the discount (3% to 8%) of the sale to the bank.

- When doing an out-of-state show, you can take the checks to the banks they are drawn on to make sure they are good.

- You can cash checks locally if you need money for travel expenses.

Most bad checks are written on new accounts. The biggest percentage of them will have check numbers from 0 to 300. If you have doubts about a person, ask for a driver's license and a current phone number. Write the numbers on the top of the check and on the sales invoice. I have been fortunate. I have never received a bad check for one of my pieces. Mostly, I never even ask for an ID, just a phone number.

State sales tax

Almost every state requires you to collect and pay a tax on each sale that you make. Some show producers include the state requirements in the application procedure. If not, contact the state you will be showing in several months in advance about getting a temporary permit. They will send you a rate chart for the asking. Sometimes they have local tax employees going from booth to booth collecting estimates of your projected sales tax payments for the rest of the show. In some states, they expect you to abide by an honor system and mail in the computed tax amount after the show. Legally, states can close you down and fine you for non-payment of sales tax owed. Though, I've never heard of it happening to a craftsperson.

How to keep track of shows

Use the form in Figure 4.0 on the next page to record information about each show you do. After you have done three or four shows, you start to forget details about a show you should remember for next year. Information on each sale is useful for tracking performance of different items, colors and fibers. See Chapter 11 for how to make a marketing plan based on past sales activities.

Other tips for having a better show

- Be prepared to wrap up the sales transaction as soon as possible. At craft shows, the more time you spend with one customer, the easier it is for another one to walk away. Have bags handy to put the purchased item in.

- You will need a small space on a table to carry out the sales transactions. This will be where the customer can comfortably write a check or sign a credit card sales slip. Keep extra pens around. They inevitably disappear.

- Keep a receipt book for customers requesting one. By writing a receipt for every sale, you have a physical record and a copy to give to the customer. Later, you can enter the information on the sales reports when you are evaluating the show.

- Have a supply of brochures or flyers about you and your craft to give with each sale or inquiry.

Figure 4.0 Craft show sales report

Craft Show Sales Report						
Date: 10/4/90	Show/City: Boulder City		Booth location: central		Type show: craft	
Travel Time: 10 hrs	In/Out?: outside	Weather: hot	# of years shown: 2		Crowd: good	
Booth Fee: $195	Auto: $20	Motel: $40	Electricity:		Insurance:	
Fixtures:	Food: $25	Parking:	Other:		Total Exp: $280	
Qty	Item	Fiber Contents	Colors	Weaver	Price	Total
1	jacket	wool/moh.	dark mix	J	350	350
1	scarf	mohair	dark mix	J	65	65
1	ruana	silk	blue	J	250	250
1	cocoon	cot/rayon	blk/gold	J	165	165
1	ruana	cotton	red	A	145	145
1	blouse	silk	pastels	J	95	95
1	scarf	wool	green/gold	D	40	40
Comments, and what to do next year:				Subtotal Sales:		1,130
bring more light weight pieces; very warm weather; good show				Less Discounts:		
				Total Sales:		1,130
				Expenses:		280
				% of Expenses to Sales:		25%

- Bring extra ones, fives and tens for making change. Keep your money in a belt concealed under your clothing. Never show large amounts of cash at the shows, or motels you stay at when traveling. In larger cities, be extra careful when leaving the show to hide your money.

- Consider buying a carpet remnant or rug for your booth. It looks good and gives you and your customers some relief from concrete floors at indoor shows.

- Wear comfortable clothing; something you have made is the best promotion you can give your work. Also get a pair of comfortable sneakers.

- Bring a lunch. The fewer times you leave your booth, the better chance of making sales. If you have someone to help you, it's easier to take breaks.

- Get a toolbox to keep emergency tools and supplies like scissors, electrical and duct tape, hammer, nails, pliers, screwdrivers, string or flexible wire and spare parts for fixtures or booths. Keep a small box with needle, thread, crochet hook and scissors for unexpected snags or just discovered mistakes. Include it in your toolbox.

- For indoor shows, bring long extension cords, power strips and clamp-on lights with bulbs. The better your lighting, the more you will sell.

- Make a checklist of the above items and go over it before you leave for the show.

The more shows you do, the more often you will be approached by store owners looking for new merchandise. The next section helps you answer questions about selling to stores and what to expect from large trade shows.

Section 2

Moving Into the Big Time

Chapter 5   How to Sell to Stores & Galleries

How to approach stores

A direct approach is the easy way to get your work into stores or galleries. In most cities, I have had good results simply walking into a store and introducing myself to the owner or manager. I explain that I'm a weaver and ask if they would be interested in looking at a few pieces of my work. Most of the time, they will look right then. It's easy for them to say *"no"* on the phone, but once you're standing in front of them, they figure *"what the heck, show me what you have."* I never walk in with the pieces however, it's too presumptuous and unprofessional, and it only takes a minute to go back to the car.

Unless you have a specific appointment, avoid approaching stores on a Monday, Friday, or weekend. The best times are mornings, in the middle of the week. Store owners are too busy or too tired in the afternoon, and they are often gone on weekends.

The bigger the shop the more likely they will want to make an appointment for another day. Stay flexible enough to work with their time frame. Never attempt to push your schedule on them.

If you're going to travel to sell to stores, send an introductory letter, brochure, photos and fabric swatches ahead of time. Call about a week to 10 days after you send the packet to confirm that it was received and set up an appointment. If they will see you at a specific time, then you know you will meet with the person who makes the buying decisions.

> *Every time I wove a special piece to wear at shows or special events, someone would see it and 'just die if they couldn't have it', so I always gave in and sold it to them. Finally, I'd had enough of not being able to say "no." I spent three days weaving, sewing and knitting the finishes to a special sweater that I promised I would never sell. Unfortunately, whenever I did a show or walked into a shop, they wanted pieces like it. This would have been fine except for the tremendous amount of inventory I had of already completed work not as detailed as the special sweater. Nevertheless, this is one sure way to find out about pieces you should be making.*

What to do when you get there

Here are some tips to help you when you make presentations to stores. It's important that your personal appearance, promotional material and the way in which your work is shown be clean and professional.

1) Wear something you've made. Weave a suit or wrap that reflects the kind of work you will sell to stores.

2) Don't be late or early. If you don't show up on time, what do you think they will imagine about delivery of your products? If you get there before they're ready for you, you will likely cause irritation.

3) Before you leave home, check over your sample pieces for lint, loose threads, open seams, wrinkles and labels. Carry a small repair kit if you go on the road. Include a travel iron, scissors, thread, sewing needle, knitting needle, seam ripper, measuring tape and a few bobbins of yarn.

4) Have your price lists, brochures and business cards ready to give out. You also will need photos of your work and fabric samples. Brochures are expensive, but they say 'professional'. See Chapter 13 for more on promotional material.

5) Find an attractive carrying bag for going into stores. Cardboard boxes and garbage bags present a poor image. I took some beautiful tapestry fabric and made a travel bag for protecting my woven clothing. If you sell rugs or flat items, make a large, handwoven duffle bag in which to carry them.

Personalizing the relationship with the owner is an important part of building a wholesale business. This creates a comfortable feeling on both sides. It also helps when it comes to the matter of getting paid. If you have a positive rapport with an owner, they'll be more prompt with payment of invoices.

Finding stores

You may not have to look far to find wholesale accounts. It's inevitable that you will be approached by store owners at craft shows; craft fairs are the obvious place for them to look for new merchandise.

If you want your business to grow, follow up these leads with a phone call. Make an appointment to meet with the owner and give a presentation. Even if four out of five don't turn out, one good store account can provide steady sales for a long time. When you establish wholesale accounts, keep in touch with them. Sales will increase in the times you make more personal visits or telephone calls with the owners.

When I was first approached by a shop owner, I was selling ruanas, shawls and sweaters at a craft show. She told me she owned several stores in the Midwest for larger size women's clothing. My handwoven ruanas appealed to her and she asked me to call her the following week with wholesale prices and delivery times.I put her card away, without giving it much consideration. I thought that at that time, I was having better sales at craft shows than I could from working with stores. I regretted this attitude later, when show sales slowed. By then, I couldn't find her card or remember her company's name. After this, I was careful to follow up every lead. This resulted in several steady wholesale accounts that allowed me more time to weave at home and netted almost as much per piece as I was clearing from selling at craft shows.

Another time, my wife Dianne and I were in Boulder, Colorado exploring the possibility of joining an artist's co-op gallery. The size of the gallery, its annual sales and location looked appealing. The amount of weaving on display, however, discouraged us; 6 or 7 local weavers were represented with a substantial inventory of scarves, clothing, rag rugs and wall hangings. Walking down the street, we found two more such ventures; co-op galleries for local artists were definitely catching on. Again, we found more local weavers.

Thinking there was just too much competition, we gave up our search and went to lunch. Coming out of the cafe, Dianne noticed a shop that sold Santa Fe style gifts. We went in and saw a variety of moderately expensive south-western arts and crafts, but no weaving. We were about to leave, when I suddenly thought to try to sell the owner on the idea of carrying our work since she already carried the Santa Fe style.

She was interested! Though, only if we would leave pieces on consignment, which I consider a low priority. I was anxious however, to test this market so close to outlets where local weavers were deeply entrenched.

In the first month, nothing sold. After my first call back to the store, I neglected to check with them again, being busy with shows and other projects. At the end of two months, I had almost forgotten the account. This was not a good move. One Saturday, the owner called to tell me she was sending a check for three pieces. She had sold the most expensive jackets we made and she wanted more things ASAP! The moral is: it pays to keep in touch with your store accounts on a regular basis, even when you think nothing is happening.

Listings of stores that buy crafts

Before you take off down the road to sell your goods, compile a list of your target accounts. You can gather names of stores in various ways.

- Yellow Pages directories for most major cities can be found in your home town library. Look under Women's Apparel, Hotels (gift stores), Airport, Museums, Interior Decorators & Designers/Suppliers, and Art Galleries. If you want to reach special retail markets like thoroughbred horse owners, look under Horse Furnishings.

- *The Official Museum Directory* by the American Association of Museums (check your library) lists the nation's museums. Address your inquiries to 'Gift Shop' so that it will go straight to the store.

- A guide that lists store buyers is *The Directory of Craft Stores* with over 700 stores, sales reps, craft co-ops, and mail order catalogs that buy crafts (see the Bibliography).

- American Craft Enterprises sells up-to-date mailing lists of the craft buyers that have attended their most recent ACC shows. Names and addresses are sent on mailing label sheets ready to use. Write or call American Craft Enterprises, PO Box 10, New Paltz, NY 12561, (800) 527-3844 or (914) 883-6100 in New York.

- *The Crafts Reports* has a 'crafts wanted' section where stores buying craft items advertise what they are looking for and the average price range.

- A mail list of 800 craft buyers rents from Karen Gamow, 14618 Tyler Foote Rd., Nevada City, CA 95959.

- To locate buyers in a particular trade, look into that industry's wholesale trade associations and publications. One of their chief objectives is providing more opportunities for suppliers and members to connect. Your library can provide you with references listing associations and trade shows.

You probably will spend more money per sale when traveling to get store accounts than you would if you were to exhibit at a wholesale trade show. Unless you are producing a large amount of inventory, though, trade shows could result in more orders than you can fill.

In the last few years, the number of retail stores that sell handcrafted items has been steadily increasing though craft sales in galleries have declined. It seems that customers are more accepting of buying fine craftwork when it is displayed in a retail environment; another increase in the number of potential markets you can sell to.

At some point, you must learn how many stores you can comfortably supply. This will depend on how much you want to produce. Chapter 11 helps you analyze your production capabilities.

Your work might be inappropriate for selling in large quantities. One-of-a-kind coats with lots of detail and finish work are sought after by high priced boutiques, but you spend days, maybe weeks, creating one piece. It is difficult to survive by exclusively trying to sell this kind of weaving because sales are infrequent. The more practical approach is to produce a line of steady selling products, establish a reliable income, and then take a week now and then to work on special one-of-a-kind projects.

Is doing wholesale business for you?

If you aren't sure about doing business with stores, the following points will help you see the whole picture.

● The wholesale price you ask will usually be 50% of what the store marks an item. Can you sell to stores and still make a profit? Use the information in Chapter 2 on pricing and figuring profit margins to learn which items will yield a profit at wholesale prices.

● Store owners will tell you what they can and can't move. This means you will be producing to suit their market. How much do you want to work for someone else?

● Develop a line of complementary products rather than offering only one or two items in a category. For example, products for the home might include blankets, rugs, placemats, pillows, etc.. For clothing, you might make 10 different kinds of garments. Buyers are more comfortable with a line of several choices. Offering a product line conveys an impression of the size and solidity of your operation.

- Store owners want to see consistency of style in your work that distinguishes your pieces from others. Look at the work of your competition and you'll see what I mean. Successful artisans develop a theme in their work.

- Some stores insist on exclusivity. They might even want you to sign an agreement that you will not sell your work anywhere else in the same city or area. Avoid such a contract, if possible. It can only limit your sales and there's no reasonable chance that one store will sell any more of your work in exchange for exclusive rights. I have skirted this issue by using another company name, with a different set of business cards, labels and hang tags. This way, if I am approached by another account in the same area, I can reputably have my work in both locations without angering either. Of course, I never tell them what I'm doing. If you set up a similar operation, be careful not to send duplicate pieces to two stores in the same town. Theoretically, you could start several 'name brands' to enter as many markets in the same city as you could handle. Check with your bank about depositing checks made out to different brand names. An added benefit of this system is you can test new color or style combinations in the same locations to see how sales compare.

- Ask for a purchase order number from a store at the time it places an order. This is especially important with large companies like department store chains where, due to the high volume of merchandise they handle, an order may be refused or questioned. A purchase order is your only proof that they placed an order. With independent stores where you have a positive relationship with the owner, there is less likelihood of this happening. Nevertheless, it is best to avoid confusion and be a business professional in your dealings.

- When shipping orders, use United Parcel Service (UPS). Stores must sign for each delivery. This is your record that they received it, in case there's a dispute. It's also easier to track lost packages through UPS than to try to find missing parcels through the postal service. If you do send something parcel post, request a return receipt, though it will add to the cost. Otherwise, there is no record of the package being received.

- Persons or companies ordering goods usually pay shipping charges. Add this amount on to the invoice when billing. Use invoices printed so that 'Freight is F.O.B. (your address)' is clearly seen. F.O.B. means 'freight on board', the point to where you, the seller pays the freight.

- Seek store accounts that buy your work outright as opposed to consignment agreements.

- Keep in touch with stores regularly; you not only find out about buying trends, you learn what the competition is producing.

- Galleries like to have copies of your resume or vitae handy for customers interested in your work. A well prepared resume will list your education, awards, teaching and speaking credits, organizations and exhibitions.

- A warning about new stores or galleries. I have been solicited at craft shows, and through the mail, by new stores or galleries appearing as co-op ventures but in fact, they rent a large building and sub-rent small partitioned spaces to individual artisans. Take the time to check a business out before you sign any rental agreements. Ask the manager for the names of other craftspersons participating so you can talk to them about the operation.

Extending credit

If a store buys your work outright more than once, they will soon expect you to allow them 30 days to pay for goods received. This is normal terms for most businesses. Selling your handwoven items wholesale may make it more difficult for you to grant payment terms because it restricts your cash flow. Also, if you can get the stores to pay upon receipt of goods, you won't have collection hassles. Your ability to establish your own terms will be based on how well your work sells.

Make your first sale to an account C.O.D. (collecting payment upon delivery). Send the store owner a blank credit application and a request for a financial statement. You can usually purchase blank application forms at your office supply store.

Ask for three references. These you should call or write with these questions: What do you make and sell? How long have you been doing business with this store? Do you extend credit terms to them? If so, for how long? Would you recommend this store for credit?

Though most persons strive for integrity in business, some have financial trouble and fall behind in paying their bills. Also, it's unwise to assume that everyone you deal with is honest. A few store owners make it a policy to take advantage of small suppliers.

What happens after you have extended credit and the account does not pay? The more time that goes by on an overdue bill, the less chance you will get your money. After 90 days of being overdue, your likelihood of collecting is 80%, after 180 days your chances drop to 50%. It's risky to extend credit to stores open for fewer than three years because most businesses fail within the first three to five years of their start-up.

Action taken by you in advance is more valuable than any efforts made after a collection problem has come up. When you are reviewing a credit application for a store, also seek information from Dun & Bradstreet. They collect data on businesses of every size. For information, write Dun & Bradstreet, Dept. 178, 1 Imperial Way, Allentown, PA 18195.

To protect yourself from possible collection problems, be on the lookout for:

- Large reorders following prompt payment on a small first few orders

- Reorders sent out before prior invoices are paid

- Buyers that seem demanding or in a rush

- Phone numbers not listed with directory assistance

- Information on credit application that you cannot confirm.

If you do a large wholesale business to the giftware industry, you can screen prospective accounts before you extend them credit through the services of Manufacturers Credit Cooperative of Plano, TX.

Member businesses agree to provide a listing of their delinquent accounts to the Cooperative monthly. Also, members receive a comprehensive listing of reported business's 90-day payment delinquencies, accounts submitted to a collection agency, insufficient funds or dishonored checks, accounts refusing COD orders after ordering, bankruptcy/closings and other useful information every month. MCC also offers pre-collection and attorney assisted collection services. Their pre-collection service can be particularly useful in getting payment without arousing animosity. To find out more about their service, write to Manufacturers Credit Cooperative, PO Box 860188, Plano, TX 75086, (214) 422-7852.

Consignment

Consigning your work means that you leave your woven items at the store without receiving payment until some time after the sale. Pieces remain your property until sold. An agreement with the details of the arrangement is usually signed by the store owner and you. See the example in Figure 6.0.

Consignment is looked on with different feelings by every craftsperson. Some say don't do consignment at all. Others have a softer attitude toward the situation. Most consignment arrangements benefit the store or gallery more than they benefit the artist. Stores get inventory at no cost to them. They also have the use of the money from the time of the sales till the time they pay the artist. Commonly, payment is made by the 15th of the following month.

My first wholesale experience was with a retail gallery carrying a variety of craft items on consignment. I was approached by the manager of the shop at a craft show. She seemed enthusiastic about having my work in their store, located on the downtown plaza of Santa Fe where thousands of tourists pass every day. I was too flattered to think that a big retail outlet would be anything but fair and business like.

I left 12 pieces on consignment. One piece sold after the first month. The store did not call me or send a check. I only found out because I had returned to the store 6 weeks later to see if anything had moved. They wrote me a check while I was there. I briefly wondered *"would they have paid if I hadn't shown up?"* Another piece was sold soon afterwards. When the agreed time for promised payment went by, I gave the manager a call. She said *"no problem, the check is on the way."* Another two weeks went by with no sign of the check. When I called again, I heard this line *"oh, sorry, our accountant is out on vacation and she's the only one who can sign the checks."* By now, it's starting to smell.

I made 6 or 7 calls over the next two months, all long distance, because I lived 90 miles away. It was truly amazing how many different excuses I received for not getting paid. A really good one was *"We're experiencing a slight cash flow problem. It should be straightened out soon."* The store sold a piece it never paid for, collected the money and did not keep it on account.

When I couldn't sleep one night because I was so angry, I saw the need for stronger action. I called the manager the next morning and said, *"Look, it's been two and a half months since you sold my piece. Every time I call, I hear a different excuse. I'm coming there this afternoon to get my money. If you don't have it ready, I'm taking my records of all the transactions to the local magistrate and filing a claim, including all my expenses put out to try to get my money."* When I arrived at the store, they wrote me a check. They acted as if I had hurt their feelings with my accusations.

A few months later, the store went bankrupt, owing several craftspersons for unpaid sales. When I told the story to a potter next to me at a crafts show, he

Figure 6.0 Sample consignment agreement

CONSIGNMENT CONTRACT

The undersigned, owner of _____ Gallery agrees that _____ (artist's name) is a consignee of the _____ Gallery, city, state. The medium/media in which the above has been accepted is weaving. The artist's work will remain the property of the artist until it is sold. The Gallery maintains an insurance policy against personal property losses, burglary, and liability. The undersigned consignee named in this contract understands and agrees that:

1. The seller shall retain a commission of 40% of list price of any article. The seller shall use the artist's recommended value as a guide for pricing articles.

2. The seller will deduct all consignment commissions from the selling price of any item and will remit the balance to the artist monthly. Checks to artists are written around the 15th of each month for sales through the last day of the previous month.

3. Consigned items will be displayed for 90 days unless the artist is notified otherwise. Upon notification, articles must be picked up within 5 days by the artist or designated agent or they shall become the property of _____ Gallery.

4. The artist does___ or does not___ wish to make articles available through the Gallery's lay-away plan.

5. Like works by an artist exhibiting at the Gallery which are for sale elsewhere in_____City shall be priced the same as the established retail price of _____ Gallery.

6. The Gallery requests that a one-week notice be given before removing any items from the Gallery.

7. The _____Gallery retains the right to accept or reject any articles presented by an artist for sale or display and further retains the right to display articles in any manner which it deems appropriate.

8. Items discounted to decorators or designers result in the discount being split between the artist and the Gallery. The amount of the discount will not exceed 10%.

9. The_____Gallery will receive 25% commission on studio sales and all other sales resulting from referral from the Gallery or as a result of exposure of the artist's work in the Gallery.

Articles are accepted by the _____ Gallery for sale subject to the terms and conditions of this contract. The artist specifically represents herself/himself as the lawful owner or agent for the owner of all consigned articles and that there are no liens, encumbrances, or payments due on any article.

This contract will be binding until such time that either party violates the terms of said agreement or until new policies demand adjustments.

_____Signature of gallery owner   _____Date

_____Signature of artist   _____Date

said "Oh yeah, them. Everybody knows they have a bad reputation for not paying." Everybody except me, the new kid on the block.

This is a good example of how talking with other craftspersons can help you know ahead of time which stores to avoid.

Are there any good reasons to consign your work? Maybe. One is that some galleries pay the artist 60% of the amount of the sale. This is 10% more than a store buying outright pays for the same piece. You may be asking "Why not raise your wholesale prices to collect the extra 10% when making the outright sale?" If your store accounts will pay the price you want, there's no problem. But, I find it confusing to jockey my prices around to fit different situations. It's also illegal. Federal Trade Commission says that any "deal" offered to one customer must be offered to all.

Every store or gallery I have consigned to has let me set the retail prices. Of course, it makes sense to discuss pricing with the owner to know how similar products are priced.

Before consigning your products, consider the following:

1) What distance is the store located from you? The farther away, the more chances of problems and the more expensive it is to ship.

2) How long has the store been in business? New stores seek work on consignment to fill their displays. They are also the most likely to have problems with cash flow and paying their suppliers.

3) Don't consign to stores that buy outright from other craftspersons. Why should you? If your work isn't good enough for them to pay for, there are plenty of other stores that will.

4) Ask other craftspeople or weavers if the store has a reputation for non-payment or late payments.

If you consign, leave at least 12 pieces on display. This isn't a problem for the store. The more pieces shown, the more you'll sell. You may choose consignment arrangements simply to get in with certain desirable shops. Remember though, you're doing them a favor. If you consign, make it a policy to do consignment in stores where you can generate positive relations with the owners.

Selling on approval

Selling on approval is an alternative to consigning that gives you, the supplier, more of an advantage. In such an agreement, you leave some number of pieces on approval for 60 to 90 days. At the end of that time, if the buyer has made sales, they pay you for those pieces and whatever they decide to keep in the store. This method lets you test stores as markets without the hassle of tying up inventory for longer periods. If your work doesn't sell, neither you, nor the owner will want to continue displaying the pieces.

Sales representatives

If you plan to do a large amount of wholesaling, you may want to investigate using sales representatives, or reps. Using reps means you can stay home and produce and let them spend the time and expense it takes to show your work to their established accounts. By using several reps, you can extend your exposure to a national audience.

They receive a commission from you (15% to 25%) on the wholesale price you are charging the stores. They expect payment from you at the end of the month, whether the store has paid for the order or not.

Supply your reps with brochures, photos of your work, samples, price lists, order blanks, and conditions of sales. Make sure you can produce the inventory that is required to fill the orders coming from more accounts. Know your production limits and keep your agents informed of delivery schedules. Don't expect to receive orders from a store or a rep when you promise delivery and can't come through.

When considering a sales rep for your products, send the individual agent or company a questionnaire. This is like asking them for their resume, which isn't a bad idea either. Ask for the following information. Follow up the references they give you of other craftspersons with a phone call or letter of inquiry asking if they would recommend them. Find out: What other artists do you represent? What is the wholesale price range of your product lines? How long have you been a sales rep (company)? How do you handle refused shipments and canceled orders? What stores do you sell to? What area of the country?

There is always the question of whether the sales rep will actually show your work. They don't have the same time and effort invested in the pieces as you do. You aren't required to sign a life-time contract with anyone. Typically, a rep will ask for a 6 to 12 month agreement. If they aren't moving your work, discontinue your arrangement and try someone else.

How do you find a sales rep?

Directory of Wholesale Reps in the Bibliography, is a comprehensive listing of reps who carry craft items. Also, check the classified ads of *The Crafts Report.*

You may prefer to establish new accounts yourself. Talking with them personally always gives you insights because owners know what sells. Once you decide to sell to stores, the next step in expanding sales is by way of large wholesale trade shows. The following chapter tells you how to find and enter these events and what to expect from them.

Chapter 6   How to Succeed at
Wholesale Trade Shows

There are trade shows for almost every industry and interest group. They
serve as outlets for the latest trends and designs in products and services
provided to any given trade. Each interest group draws buyers and users
from all over the country to these events. Who comes to wholesale craft trade
shows? Store buyers, interior decorators, architects, museum buyers, sales
reps and mail order catalog buyers.

When you're ready to expand on a large scale, wholesale shows are the
logical means. Before you sign up for one though, you should have a clear
picture of what they will require of you. You should also know how big you
want your business to grow. Information provided in this chapter will help
you make an informed choice.

A wholesale business requires the inventory, production capacity, and
ambition to expand on a national or regional scale. It means deadlines and
work schedules, selling at wholesale prices, delays in collecting payments for
orders, higher exhibit costs and hiring help to fill larger orders. It may also
mean greater prestige, sense of accomplishment, and increased income.

Large trade shows give you easy access to thousands of buyers. These buyers
are keenly aware of what sells and what doesn't in their stores. Talking to
them, you can pick up invaluable guidance for designing and producing your
handwoven products. You can also use the trade shows to learn what trends
are coming in specific market groups, like jewelry, interiors or fashion.

Trade shows make it easy to develop relations with store owners in a
friendly, relaxed way. Some of these personal connections can last for many
years.

Big shows can mean big orders. Many craft exhibitors get enough orders from these shows to last all year. One of the larger producers of craft trade shows is Wendy Rosen Shows. They put on several wholesale shows a year in Boston, MA, San Francisco, CA, and Philadelphia, PA, and they sponsor two shows for decorative accessories at the International Home Furnishings Market in High Point, North Carolina.

Another large show producer is American Craft Enterprises. *The Crafts Report* listed the following information about the ACC craft fair in Baltimore, 1991. There were 900 exhibitors, 480 of whom reported their sales. Total wholesale sales were projected at over $5,000,000. Fiber retail sales were $445,680. Fiber wholesale totals were in excess of $550,000. For all media, average booth sales came to $12,149 wholesale and $4,944 retail.

At these events, you can see what other artists in your medium produce for the wholesale trade. Don't be discouraged by the number of competing exhibitors. The more products you see similar to yours, the greater the likelihood of your success because they have proven the marketability.

Entry requirements

A major determinate in a craftsperson's acceptance in these shows is previous experience as a wholesale supplier. If you apply to them, have the names of stores you have done business with and other wholesale shows where you have exhibited. Producers spend much time and money to put on shows to attract buyers from all over the country. They expect you to supply accounts on time and in a professional manner.

Laura Rosen, vice-president of the Wendy Rosen Shows explained the programs they offer to help new exhibitors wishing to enter the wholesale market. Each Rosen show designates an area called 'Premier Designers' to draw attention to new artisans. If you're accepted into the show, this can be a great boost for your first exhibit at a major trade event. The Rosen Shows also offer repeating exhibitors a guaranteed entry without going through the application process.

Workshops and seminars are presented on preparing promotional material, display design and wholesale practices. Rosen Shows also publish *CraftED* an educational marketing kit for craftspeople. Topics included are: printing and promotion, direct mail, advertising, trade shows, designing exhibits, credit and collection, customer service, and a press list of major publications. This kit may be ordered for around $10 directly from them at this address: Wendy Rosen Shows, 3000 Chestnut Avenue, Suite 300, Baltimore, MD 21211.

Another publication available from the Rosen Agency is *NICHE, The Magazine for Progressive Retailers*. This quarterly magazine is mailed to 20,000 craft and specialty retailers and an additional 5,000 copies are distributed at each of Rosen's shows. Display advertising for craftspersons is available and is a good way to let the buyers know about you before they arrive at the show.

Which shows should I do?

Your products can be marketed through several different wholesale trade markets. Craft and gift trade shows can work for most items you make. Fashion shows are a targeted way for marketing clothing and accessories. Interior designers and architects attend trade shows for products used in designing home and office decor.

There is a list of the major craft trade show promoters in the Appendix. You can also find listings of shows in craft periodicals and weaving magazines. Write them for their schedule and fees. For a listing of trade shows by industry, see the *Trade Shows and Professional Exhibit Directory* in your library. Also, check out the *Tradeshow & Exhibit Manager*, 1150 Yale St., Suite 12, Santa Monica, CA 90403. Another directory of over 11,000 trade shows is *TradeShows & Exhibits Schedule,* 633 Third Avenue, New York, NY 10017, ($170.00).

It's important that you find the right show for what you're selling. If the show doesn't reach a receptive market for your product, the financial and emotional disappointment could be a serious blow. Research the show carefully. Attend the event in person, talk to past exhibitors, read reviews of the event in trade magazines like *The Crafts Report*. Call the show management. It's in their best interests too that you find the appropriate show for your products. It's worth an exploratory trip to see what happens at these events. Managers are likely to give you a guest pass if you call in advance and explain you wish to attend to evaluate the show.

If you already have wholesale accounts, ask them which shows they attend that might work well for you. What do they look for when they go there? What kind of displays draw their interest?

In researching a trade show, find out the following:

● Is this show going to attract the type of buyers that want your product? How many attend the show? What was last year's sales and attendance? This information should be available from the management when you request an application. If it isn't, call and talk to the manager before you apply.

- Does the show conflict with another larger trade show elsewhere? Sometimes promoters tie their show dates and locations closely to draw more attendees. List all trade show schedules and compare the dates.

- What will be the total cost of doing the show? Booth rental fees on the larger trade shows will cost anywhere from $500 to $1,500 up and $100 to $300 more for corner or specific spots. How big is the space? How are cancellations handled? If you choose to ship your display, what will the freight costs be?

- What do you get for your money? Is electricity, backdrops, tables, chairs, parking and unloading fees included in the rental or are they a separate charge? Must union electricians and dock workers be paid for set-up? Some exhibition centers in larger cities are run by unions with stringent rules. Silly as it seems, you can't plug in your own electricity, you must pay a union electrician to do it. If the Teamsters union is in control, you must allow them to load and unload your booth. Unless management lets you carry it in by hand, expect to pay a couple of hundred dollars extra for these 'services'.

- Where is the show held? Is this the first time in a new location? Location changes often affect attendance. How easy is unloading and setting-up?

- Can you produce the inventory to fill large orders? Can you deliver on time? You'll be taking orders to ship at later dates, so it's important that you know in advance the amount of orders you can fill and when you can fill them. Normally some buyers cancel, but you can't know how many. It's far better to stop taking orders when you reach your fulfillment level than to promise delivery and then fail to do so. Word does get around. Once you get a reputation for non-delivery of orders, it's hard to prove to them you won't do it again.

- Can you afford to sell to larger chain stores that require payment terms of 30 to 60 days? How will it affect your cash flow if a large account delays or fails to pay for an even longer time? Can you continue to buy yarn, exhibit at shows, pay employees and other operating costs?

- Are you willing to hire employees to keep up with the demands of increased production? How much of your time are you willing to spend managing others?

- *Do you want a bigger business?* I saved this one for last so you could read the list of what's facing you before you think about this important, but no longer simple question.

Exhibiting at a major wholesale trade show isn't for the shy. Besides the high cost of booth rental, trade fairs require intense personal stamina and enthusiasm. Demands go far beyond the more relaxed, local art and craft shows.

Advance planning

Trade shows take careful planning, months in advance. As with craft shows, it helps to make a list and check off items as you have them ready.

- As mentioned before, attend the show before you apply. Talk to the management and other exhibitors about what to expect.

- Apply for the show early, like 6 months to a year. This increases your chances of being accepted.

- Advertise in trade publications of the groups interested in your products. *NICHE* is a mixed media publication that goes to craft buyers attending the Rosen Shows. *The Crafts Report* publishes a special show section before each of the bigger shows with advertising available to craftspersons.

- Send out direct mail letters to previous customers and prospective new accounts. Include reviews and feature articles about you. Tell them your booth location and mention new products you'll be showing. Follow up the mailing with phone calls. This method is essential to get buyers to visit your booth.

- Exhibit center lighting is never enough to effectively show your display. Bring extra lighting, even if you think the hall is well lit. Halogen bulbs create more balanced illumination than incandescent (adds reddish tint) or fluorescent (adds bluish tint) bulbs.

- Order tables, chairs and electricity when you apply. They cost more when ordered at the show. Provide extra chairs for buyers to sit in, but don't *you* sit if a buyer is in your booth.

- Have photo portfolios, catalogs, brochures, price list with terms, business cards and order forms typeset and printed professionally; allow at least a month for this process. Make sure your products are tagged, with wholesale prices clearly marked. Display the informational and promotional literature neatly on a small table where you can write orders and hand out your materials.

- Have flyers with your location mapped out, distributed to buyers when they first enter the show. Also, write your booth number on your business cards and other hand-outs. Give them to buyers walking through the show, so they can find you again when they return to make their orders.

- Buy attractive carpet with padding to cover the floor of your booth. Buyers get sore feet walking on the concrete floors of big exhibit halls.

- Arrange your travel details well in advance, like flight and hotel reservations. Many of the buyers attending use the hotel designated by the trade show, you can make valuable contacts by staying there, though it may seem more costly than staying in a motel.

- Get exhibitor's insurance for the days of the show and transit time to and from to protect yourself from losses or damages. Ask the company you currently use. See Chapter 10 under 'Insurance' for sources.

- If you ship your booth, carry some pieces of your work, brochures, order forms, and price lists with you. That way, if your booth display doesn't arrive, you will at least have something to show.

- Flame-proof your exhibit materials such as table covers and fabric backdrops. Most cities have strict regulations enforced by fire marshals inspecting each booth.

- Apply for a Dun & Bradstreet number to establish your business reliability. For information, write Dunn & Bradstreet, Dept. 178, 1 Imperial Way, Allentown, PA 18195.

- Make an office supply kit including: scissors, tape, staplers, pens, hammer, peg hooks and anything else you can think of that you might possible use at a show.

- You might also bring some large pieces of fabric to throw over your display at closing time. Though they wouldn't stop a thief, covers will remove temptation from easy sight.

- Make sure your display is sturdy by setting it up at home first.

- It is to your advantage to know all the rules before you arrive. Show managers provide a regulations and guidelines book for exhibitors. Read it a couple of times and follow instructions to the letter. Don't hesitate to call them with questions about procedures. They want everything to run as smoothly as you do.

Booth displays at trade shows

An average trade show attendee spends as few as 30 seconds at a booth before moving on, so your exhibit has to catch their eye quickly. Displays used for an outdoor craft show will most likely be inappropriate in a trade show. Indoor booths are typically separated by pipe and drape curtains about 3 ft. high on the sides and 8 ft. high in the back. Drapes and pipe are usually provided as part of your booth charge.

Buyers should feel free to enter and look at your work. You will make more sales if you build an exhibit that represents how a store or gallery might display the pieces; buyers then have no problem imagining your work in their store.

You can gain useful insights into effective displays by looking at all of the booths in the show, not just the other artists in your medium. Watch to see why some booths attract interest and always have a crowd. If you feel at a loss for designing a booth, and you cannot visit a trade show, most major cities will have 'Display Designers' in the Yellow Pages. Check out their catalogs and floor models for ideas.

If your booth location seems too far from the main stream of browsers, ask the show manager when you first arrive about trading. As in the art and craft shows, there are always last minute cancellations. You can guarantee your-self a better location when you first apply by paying an additional fee for a corner spot. These are the better selling spaces because buyers can see you from two different directions. Prior exhibitors get first pick on locations.

Getting orders at a trade show

Casual conversation is your easiest means of breaking the ice with buyers. After you introduce yourself, ask a question that requires a response to draw them into conversation, like *"Do you sell many handwovens?"* If they are wearing a name tag, address them by name. Ask them about their business. Find out what their needs are. They will tell you if your product will move in their store. Be sure to give them your brochure, business card, price list, order form and credit application. Do this even with buyers not willing to order at the time. Thank them for stopping by your booth, shake hands and give them a smile. Many buyers wait till the show is over to place orders. Follow up every lead with a note or phone call expressing pleasure in meeting them and include thanks, even if they didn't place an order. They will remember you as a person as much as they remember the quality of your products.

A good summation of how to have a successful show is 1) make your booth location known to your buyers and easy to locate, 2) make your products easy to see and touch with plenty of product information, and 3) make yourself accessible at all times. If you want to do trade shows, the best single piece of advice is to attend two or three and see what they are about, before you sign up for one. A good guide to doing trade shows is *Exhibit Marketing* by Edward Chapman. Also *The Crafts Report* frequently writes features about doing wholesale exhibits.

Chapter 7   How to Sell Through Mail Order

Mail order offers attractive benefits as a home based business. Orders and payments arrive in the mail, you fill the order and send it to the customer. You do most of your business without leaving home. This chapter describes techniques that can be applied to selling direct to the consumer or to wholesale store accounts.

Success in mail order, or any other marketing effort, comes by targeting the particular groups of customers that want what you are selling. You then focus your time and resources on selling to this group(s). This may sound simple, but many small businesses waste their small, precious capital resources trying to sell goods to persons who have no proven interest in their product.

Mail order, sometimes known as direct response, is a science, complete with its own statistics and techniques. By following the rules, you can accurately predict in a short time whether doing business by mail is going to work for you. It is important to test a sampling of your target audience with your offer before you spend money on a large campaign. Responses are predictable within a given range. If your ad generates a profit, or at least breaks even, you may decide to 'roll out' with more ads to larger audiences.

There are several methods of marketing through mail order. Only a few media, however, offer a chance of successful response for handwoven and most craft products. Three media most likely to generate sales of these items are 1) direct mail, 2) catalogs offering handcrafted products and 3) magazine ads, display and classified. Other ways of getting direct response like television, radio and billboard advertising would be a 'shotgun' approach, too expensive for the audience you wish to reach.

Direct mail

You probably have received several direct mail solicitations yourself. They often consist of a three to four page personalized letter promoting a product for sale by mail. In addition, they usually offer a gift, quantity discount and a money back guarantee.

Often, your name is on a list compiled of persons who purchased or asked about specific products. Companies and mailing list brokers make extra income renting the names of persons who buy their products to other companies wishing to sell to these 'known' purchasers.

To find the names of mail list brokers, check the appendix of any mail order business start-up book in your library. List brokers will send you a catalog of the types of lists they rent.

It's difficult, if possible at all, to locate a list of proven buyers of particular craft items. You don't need to rent one anyway. Since craft shows draw the persons most likely to buy handcrafted work, you know that almost everyone attending is a potential customer. Start your own in-house mailing list from craft shows customers and others who have previously bought your work. Be sure to include those persons who showed an interest in your weaving, even if they didn't buy.

Your own customer list will provide your most profitable source of names. With such a list, you can make a direct mail offer of your products that can result in additional sales.

An effective way to make such an offer is to write a personalized letter to each of your customers. By using a word processing program on a personal computer, you can insert merge codes throughout the letter that will place the customer's name wherever you wish to address them personally. These personal letters get more responses than a standard form offer sent to "Dear Customer."

A good product may not need much help when offered in a direct mail offer. Yet, many parts of a sales offer can be made more effective in motivating the customer to act. To secure the best possible response from an offer, include as many as possible of the following elements:

● Stress the benefits of the product to the user. Make it clear why they should buy from you. Capture their interest with this benefit from the beginning of the offer.

● Personalize the letter. Use the person's name in the salutation and elsewhere in the letter, if possible. Write in a friendly style without long sentences or paragraphs. **Bold** or <u>underline</u> important points.

● Place a time limit on the offer, such as: *'This offer good till November 1st'*. Offer a discount if the order is received before the deadline. Offer a discount for multiple purchases like: *'Buy 4, get 1 free.'*

● Guarantee customer satisfaction. Offer to return their money if not totally satisfied with the product. Stand behind your guarantee.

● Give the customer the option of paying with a credit card. Make it easy to order with the option of ordering now and being billed later.

● Offer a gift for ordering now. For example, a pen with your business name and logo inscribed.

● Ask the customer for the order. Include an order form and a return envelope to make it easy for the customer to order. Tell them exactly how to choose the product they are ordering, how much money to send, where to send it to, and leave plenty of room for their name and address. Many mail order professionals consider the order form to be the most important part of the offer.

● Include testimonials of what others have said about your products. Many of your customers will happily allow you to use their satisfied comments in your sales efforts. However, send them a request for permission with a place for their signature, before you use their words.

● Point out details that establish you as a unique and qualified source. What are your credentials? How long have you been a weaver? What makes your work different? What special techniques or materials do you use?

● Add a P.S. at the end of the letter that repeats the chief benefit of your offer or product. Postscripts are the part of your letter most read.

● If possible, follow the letter with a phone call. A direct mail offer followed by a personal call has been known to double the normal number of paid responses.

Save advertisements sent to you through the mail and ads that you see in magazines and keep them in a folder. Make this your 'swipe file'. Because mail order is highly competitive, most of the ads you receive will be good examples to emulate. Check the direct mail pieces sent to you for the items mentioned above. You will find most of these offers include many of them.

Direct mail expenses

Is direct mail worth the expense? Keep track of the cost of designing and printing your promotional material, your time and the cost to mail it. Add them up. If sales from the mailing generate enough income to pay the expenses and give you a profit, it's worth your while to develop the mail order end of your business. A ballpark figure for the cost of an average mailing to 1,000 names is between $300 and $400.

You can test your product for response and see what happens. If you only break even, you are, at least, generating more name recognition for your business.

If your mailing list contains over 200 names and you foresee mailing more than three or four times a year, you can save money by buying a bulk rate mail permit from the post office. You will need to mail over 750 pieces per year to generate a savings. Annual fee for the permit is around $75. Typical bulk rate for a first class letter mailed for .29, is .19.

Mail order experts say that you can expect 1% to 3% return on direct mail efforts to a list of names with a general interest in whatever you are trying to sell. Returns can be from 5% to 10% if the offer is mailed to a group that has proven its interest by previous purchase or inquiry. I once received an 11% response from a well produced offer sent to 100 names of proven purchasers. When following up the mailing with another letter and a phone call, the response jumped to 17%.

Did I make a profit? I spent $35 to produce the personalized letters, including the cost of the paper. Price of postage was $40. Phone calls came to about $25. Project time involved about 5 hours that I valued at $15 per hour. That's a total cost of $175 for everything. Price of my product was $25 and I sold 17. Cost in producing and shipping the product was $4 per piece. 17 time $4 equals $68. Total income was $425. Total expenses were $243. $425 minus $243 equals a gross profit of $182. So yes, it was worth doing.

Catalog sales

Success of catalogs is in part, based on their ability to offer unique items unattainable from another source. Expenses involved in producing a catalog in small quantities make the project infeasible for a small business just starting out. You need several thousand customers willing to buy your products to justify the expense. An alternative is to find existing mail order catalogs carrying similar items. If you order something from one mail order catalog, you start receiving every related catalog because they buy and sell each other's customer lists.

Once you find the catalogs you want to see your work in, write them a letter of introduction, include your brochure or pictures of your work and your prices. After about a week, follow the letter with a phone call. If the catalog producer decides to accept your work, it is worth discussing their pricing experiences with similar items. You are selling wholesale to the catalog company as you would to a store, receiving 50% of the retail price. You may run into some catalogs that only take products on consignment.

Many catalogs will drop ship orders. This means they take the orders, either by phone or mail and then send you the quantity, name and address of the customer along with payment. You ship the product directly to the purchaser. Catalog companies do not usually have the space to handle the inventories of all the items they advertise.

It may not be easy to find a single catalog that would be appropriate for all crafts. Products for the home are the most likely candidates for home catalog sales, but shawls and scarves appear in clothing catalogs as well. Always obtain a sample of the catalog first. You'll know quickly whether it's appropriate for your work. Here are some directories of catalogs to look at. Another possible source is *The Crafts Report*. See your library for:

- *The Directory of Craft Shops & Galleries:* contains listings of shops and catalogs seeking handcrafted work, from The Front Room Publishers, PO Box 1541, Clifton, NJ 07015.

- *The Catalog of Catalogs II*, published by Woodbine House, 5615 Fishers Lane, Rockville, MD 20852

- *Directory of Mail Order Catalogs*, by Grey House Publishing, Pocket Knife Square, Lakeville, CT 06039

- *The Wholesale-by-Mail Catalog*, by Harper Collins Publishers, 10 E. 53rd St., NY, NY 10022

Classified ads

Classified ads appear in most major magazines toward the end of the publication. Rates, usually by the word, vary according to the circulation. More readers equal higher ad rates. This is true for display ads, also. It is difficult to generate sales of items priced more than $5 in classified ads. Higher priced products are often marketed in two steps. That is, the classified ad will offer 'free details' and if the reader responds, a direct mail packet is sent to them. This is an inexpensive way of building a mailing list of persons who prove they have an interest in your product.

Marketing handwovens this way is difficult because so often the sale of the work depends on the customer's seeing and touching the piece before they will buy. If you make smaller items like placemats, earrings, pillows, or Christmas ornaments, consider a color brochure with photos and description of the products. This brochure, along with a price list and a letter about your business could then be sent to persons responding to your ads.

For a craftsperson, newspaper ads to sell products are a waste of money. Because each issue is available daily, the paper is usually glanced through once and then trashed. Magazines on the other hand, are often kept for months after purchase. I have received responses to ads placed in magazines over four years after the issue when the ad first appeared. The majority of your responses, however, will come in the first two months.

Display ads

Display ads are the larger ads appearing throughout a periodical, either with color, or black and white photos. These ads aren't cheap. It is important to know that your advertising dollar will reach an audience who wants your product. A one page, full color ad run one time in a periodical like *Family Circle* costs about $90,000. They claim over 15 million women readers will see each issue. Even if you receive enough orders to pay for the ad, can you produce the inventory for thousands of buyers?

Rates drop with black and white ads and for smaller page dimensions. If you want to know a magazine's ad rates, send them a post card asking for advertising rates and circulation information. They will send you their media kit with a sample issue, rates, lay-out requirements and reader profiles.

Display ads should not be placed in magazines where no one else is running ads of similar products. The chances are good the market has been tested and did not work. If you see products like yours in such ads, however, check several back issues of that magazine at your library. Advertisements that appear in current issues in periodicals where the ad has run for a year or more, must be getting results. Most businesses will cease advertising if there is not enough response to cover expenses.

To learn if a particular magazine is suitable to advertising your product, make a list of groups of consumers that would have an interest in your item. Since the largest consumer group in the country is women, women's magazines would be the first place to look.

Don't stop your search there, though. Use your imagination and pick up copies of various titles at random, looking through the ads. Check the library for *Reader's Guide to Periodical Literature* and *The Standard Periodical Directory*. You'll find hundreds of subjects and periodicals listed. When searching through these issues, look for other advertisers of woven products like yours.

Words that sell

Advertising is a nasty word to many persons. It often means misleading the consumer into purchasing something they may not want or need. This belief makes it doubly important to design and word your ads with as much honesty as possible. Also, there are strict laws about misleading advertising. Professionals learn to seduce, not to deceive.

Certain words have proven to be more powerful to influence a reader than others. Experts employ these words to motivate the public to purchase their products. You can make use of these words too.

Among the more effective words are: new, you, now, riches, bargain, bonus, complete, easy, enjoy, exclusive, fast, free, help, love, proven, save, secret, special, success, today, yes, amazing, compare, power, quick, how to, important, last chance, magic, startling, why, when, hurry, announcing, improvement, remarkable. Books on the subject of direct marketing and mail order like John Kremer's *Mail Order Selling Made Easier* will usually list these and other response motivators.

Free publicity

You can achieve more effective coverage than that from any type of advertising through free publicity gained by feature articles. Newspapers and magazines look for newsworthy persons, ideas and events to interest their readers. See Chapter 8 for more about this no-cost exposure under promotional methods for fiber artists. A news feature tells about where to find you and your products with greater coverage than paid ads and at no expense to you.

Best times for mail offer response

Responses will vary depending on when the offer appears. Certain months of the year yield better results from mail order offers than others. If you watch your own mail, you'll see more catalogs and offers coming in the first months listed than at any other times. Unfavorable times are in November of an election year, during highly publicized events or national disasters, or in the generally poorer response months at the bottom of the following list. Here are the months in order of their response success according to many experts. Results of your offer will be better in the months listed first and become progressively slower as you mail at the other times. Months in order of response from good to worse:

1) January
2) February
3) October
4) August
5) November
6) September
7) December
8) March
9) July
10) April
11) May
12) June

Repetition of an offer also increases response. One expert advises making 7 approaches to a customer over eighteen months. Each offer should be different to avoid getting trashed immediately. The consistent action of putting your message in front of your customer is more likely to get a response than a single attempt. If you don't intend or have the resources to repeat your offer several times in various ways, you may be disappointed in the results.

A note about mail order

A mail order operation for any business should be carefully considered. The advantage is that it's a highly measurable way of doing business. Statistics and laws run true for most products marketed by mail. If you want to learn all about direct mail selling, read *Building a Mail Order Business* by William Cohen and *Mail Order Selling Made Easier* by John Kremer. These books offer some of the most useful advice on the subject. They include lots of examples of product offerings and marketing plans for tracking reponses.

Chapter 8   How To Avoid Becoming
a Starving Fiber Artist

Fiber or woven art can take form in wall hangings, tapestries, dimensional sculptures, or other media. Purchasers include corporations, hotels, banks, hospitals, law firms, airports, public buildings, museums, foundations, interior designers, individuals, church groups and others. One source mentioned later in this chapter, sells mailing lists of over 650 corporations that buy art.

Interior designers are a good market for a craftsperson to begin selling to because they frequently use local artisans. When you have successfully accomplished smaller projects for them, you find yourself getting more and larger commissions.

Corporate opportunities offer even bigger financial awards and new design challenges. You work in large, beautiful spaces where your art will be viewed by hundreds, maybe thousands daily. Your remuneration is good and guaranteed by contract, usually with partial payment in advance.

It takes hard work to complete a large commission. Corporate commissions involve months of intense effort including research, planning, promotion, financing, contracts, construction of the piece, shipping and installation. Groups like those listed above buy art to beautify what is often, otherwise lifeless space, creating better places to work, play, rest or pray. Companies also wish to project an image of pride and sophistication through an art piece and give the employees something to relate to besides cold, empty areas. Some companies feel that employees are more motivated by the addition of art to their work environment.

Grants and funding

Grants offer immediate funding for artists to develop their creative work without worrying about paying their bills. Though competition is intense, grants and study fellowships could give you the financial boost you need to get going.

An inexpensive means of finding out about appropriate funding programs for you is to call the Visual Artist Information Hotline, 1-800-232-2789. For no charge, they will send you information on funding sources, insurance, legal assistance, art colonies/residencies, public art programs and other services for visual artists. They will also send you a catalog of books by the American Council for the Arts with several excellent resources about available grants and how to apply for them, among many other subjects.

The Foundation Center publishes *The Foundation Grants Index* with over 55,000 grant descriptions ($125). They also publish *Foundation Fundamentals: A Guide for Grantseekers* ($19.95) and several other grant resources. For a free catalog, call (800) 424-9836 or write The Foundation Center, 79 Fifth Ave., NY, NY 10003. Also, write to the National Endowment for the Arts and request grant program information. National Endowment for the Arts, 1100 Pennsylvania Ave., NW, Room 710, Washington, DC 20506, (202) 682-5448.

Beyond the financial benefits of winning a grant, the award serves to identify the artist as newsworthy. This helps build a reputation and stimulate demand for the artist's work. Other ways of increasing demand can be accomplished through promotional materials, exhibitions, competitions, teaching, publicity from media coverage, reviews of previous commissions, and advertising.

Promotion for the fiber artist

Promotion is important to any business success. You can't ignore public relations hoping that some big name art columnist will discover you and make you famous. Artist's success is more often than not, self-made. Certainly some career advances can be attributed to fortunate detection by the media or generous patronage. But most become known through the practical tools at hand.

1) Promotional material: First, create a portfolio. It should convey a summary of your awards, exhibitions and education, and a photographic presentation of previous works. A portfolio should include a resume or vitae to provide the reader with written documentation of your expertise. In initial interviews, a photo portfolio is a quick and impressive way to present your work to a project group. Include pictures of at least 15 to 20 pieces.

Consider designing high quality brochures as a means of providing a one page summation of your achievements, education and one or more photos of your best pieces. Artist brochures can use the same sales tactics of the production weaver's promotional materials, though the emphasis should be on one or two exceptional works and mention of awards. If you can pick up some brochures of artists at local galleries, they will give you some ideas for designing your own. The successful brochure will include professional ad-quality photos and information on how you can be contacted.

Designers and architects are used to looking at the best quality photo advertising in their search for art and functional woven pieces. This means your brochure or ad must compete with major home furnishing suppliers who spend thousands on advertising. Costs of your promotional materials will not be cheap, but effective promotional material conveys staying power. See Chapter 12 for more ideas.

2) Exhibitions: It may take some time to choose the galleries you want to work with. Count on showing twelve to twenty of your pieces many times and talking with several owners. When you and a gallery do decide to work together, they become your agent. A gallery's fee upon selling your work ranges from 30% to 50%. Galleries put on many exhibitions a year to draw customers in to see new works by artists and generate sales. The moment your work appears in a gallery, the show lends you prestige. You must then make use of the flare of public attention to instill your name and work in the minds of prospective customers and hopefully, art critics. Exhibitions lead to reviews and feature articles, an avenue of promotion explored later.

Exhibition notices appear in the periodicals mentioned below. You can also register as an artist with such groups as those listed in this chapter, your state arts council, museums, galleries, and university art schools. These groups send out mailings of upcoming exhibitions. To find museum exhibitions, see *The Official Museum Directory* by the American Association of Museums, in your library.

When placing woven art in temporary or permanent exhibitions, careful attention should be paid to the manner of display. An excellent aid for the fiber artist is *Textiles As Art* by Lawrence Korwin, 333 N. Michigan Ave., Chicago, IL 60601 ($29.95). Mr. Korwin is a textile artist, collector and consultant. He is also a graduate mechanical engineer, designer, American Society of Interior Designers member and on the national advisory committee of Arts International. His book contains some stunning photos of traditional and contemporary textile art and important sections on safely mounting and framing pieces, positioning, lighting, care and maintenance. This is a useful resource, if you do only one exhibition a year.

3) Competitions: Nothing sells like a winning reputation. Competitions stimulate the drive to excel, though submitting your best work to the opinions of others can create tension and frustration. But when you win, that resume just keeps looking better and the dollar value of your work gets bigger and bigger. Better known events offer larger awards and esteem for the winner. There are national and regional exhibitions and competitions especially for fiber arts. These events are sponsored by organizations that aim to help further the promotion of the art form through increasing contact and information between artist and interested purchasers. Shows, conferences, and competitions are announced in *The Crafts Report, American Craft Magazine, Handwoven, Weavers, Fiberarts, Shuttle Spindle & Dyepot* and the publications of the following groups:

- International Tapestry Network (ITNET), PO Box 203228, Anchorage, AK 99520. An organization that aims to connect tapestry artists worldwide, ITNET connects those working with tapestry, organizations, special interest groups and museums across the globe. Their goal is to advance tapestry as an art form through exhibits, articles, education and connecting artists with interested groups.

- American Tapestry Alliance (ATA), Rt. 1, Box 79-A, Goshen, VA 24439, (703) 997-5104. A group that is helpful for tapestry artists, they maintain a slide collection of American tapestry pieces and lists of contacts, galleries and materials suppliers. ATA sponsors shows at major galleries and exhibitions in the U.S. and Canada.

- Surface Design Association, PO Box 20799, Oakland, CA 94620. SDA aims to stimulate and improve education of surface design art forms and provide information about professional opportunities in studios, business and exhibitions.

4) Teaching: Teaching fiber art techniques is a source of building your reputation as an expert while simultaneously supplementing your income. When publications seek newsworthy information, teachers are often sought as a source of reliable of verification about techniques and skills. Teaching opportunities can be found in universities, continuing education departments, art and design schools, museums, and conventions of weaving groups. Institutional positions usually require a degree and some sort of teaching certification.

5) Free publicity: Possibly your best source of promotion is free publicity that comes as a result of reviews and feature articles of your exhibitions by art critics for newspapers or journals. Coverage you receive from a news feature will far surpass what you could purchase through advertising. It's important to remember to always let the media know where you'll be showing. Whenever you are about to exhibit your work, send a press release to the art editor of newspapers and magazines that review artwork. Many of these publications or listed in the Appendix.

Figure 8.0 on the following page shows an example of a release form editors are used to receiving. A press release should inform the publication of the who, what, where, when, why, and how of your story. The form should be cleanly typed and double spaced. Use a heading with the name and title of the editor on the first line of the upper left corner in all caps. Follow this with the name of the periodical, and then, a short title that tells something concise about your story. Include a release date. In the upper right corner, type your name and phone number. Begin the news information about 4 inches from the top of the page. Include these elements in the order of their importance to the readers of the publication: who is it about, what is the event, when is it happening, where is the show held, why is it newsworthy. Include any past awards and accomplishments. Make the information clear, concise and magnetic.

When you send a press release, write a cover letter to the publication's editor explaining the feature briefly. Also, send past reviews or articles about you along with photos of you at work. After a few days, follow up the release with a phone call to the editor to ask if they received it. Don't try to pressure them into printing it, just confirm that they got it. If they want to do a story they'll call you.

Other publicity you can seek for yourself is by submitting feature articles about your work to newspapers, newsletters, art periodicals, art and life-style magazines, radio and TV stations. Local newspapers are always ready to write a feature article on a 'resident artist of interest' or 'hometown girl/boy' that has done something newsworthy. Sometimes the results can bring dramatic rewards in future business.

To make submissions to newspapers, get in touch with the editor of the life-style or arts and crafts section. You can find out who they are by looking through issues of the paper. Read several of their articles to become familiar with their style. Ask if you can meet them to discuss a feature article that would be news of interest to their readers. Mention and compliment pieces they have previously written. It's important to present the project as a news

Fig. 8.0 Press release example

Warm Snow

Publishers

Rte. 323, PO Box 75, Torreon, NM 87061

PRESS RELEASE
TO: VICKI HARGROVE, EDITOR
NEW CRAFTS MAGAZINE

FOR FURTHER INFORMATION:
James Dillehay
505-384-5135

<u>RELEASE AT EARLIEST DATE, PLEASE</u>

IS SELF-EMPLOYMENT 'LOOMING' IN YOUR FUTURE?

Non-professional craftspeople who are thinking about quitting their day jobs and making that nail-biting leap into the crafts industry can have a comprehensive How-to manual for making money doing what they love; *WEAVING PROFITS, How to Make Money Selling Your Handwovens* by James Dillehay. This complete 200 page guide tells how to choose handcrafted products that sell and where to sell them, set prices for maximum profits, how to succeed at craft and trade shows, how to approach stores, how to sell through mail order, how to promote your work to corporations and the interior design trade, how to make effective plans for production and marketing, what to do when your work isn't selling, six spin-off businesses, and much more. Readers will find 16 chapters organized for easy reference covering over 180 important subjects. A list is included of more than 100 different handwoven products by markets. The softcover edition is 8 1/2 x 11" with extensive appendixes that give more than 280 resources of helpful organizations, wholesale suppliers, the best craft show guides, advertising media and other useful references. *WEAVING PROFITS* can be found at yarn stores or direct from the publisher for $18.95 + $3 shipping from Weaving Profits, Box 75, Torreon, NM 87061.

Author, James Dillehay, has successfully marketed his weaving since 1985. Mr. Dillehay was formerly vice-president of a chain of retail career clothing stores based in Houston, Texas. Dissatisfied with the lack of creativity in the daily corporate workplace, he left the retail business to make his living by his own hand. After learning to weave from a friend in New Mexico, he started a company and began helping other new craftspersons as well. His marketing experiences as both a handweaver and as a corporate manager are now available in *WEAVING PROFITS* the guide that explores the real-life issues a beginning craftsperson needs to tackle.

- end -

feature rather than as an attempt at free advertising. Publications want news. Their readers want to find out what's new and worth learning about.
Do you have a finished piece you haven't been able to sell? Consider the publicity value when you donate the work to a public building, hospital or community center. Notify the newspapers with a press release!

Magazines are another avenue of free publicity. Upon your request, they will provide editorial guidelines and schedules. If you have a periodical in mind, write the editor and enclose a SASE, requesting submission guidelines for writers. As with newspapers, you should familiarize yourself with the magazine by reading several recent issues.

Approach magazine editors the same way as newspapers. When you feel you know the style and type of articles they publish, write an article about yourself and what you do. Call the editor and present the basic information about your work; who would be interested; why they would want to know; what makes your work unique; how they can find the pieces; when the work is available; and how to get in touch with you. As with the press release, include favorable reviews and awards you have received. If your story has interest to their readers, the editor will tell you. Even if they aren't interested now, their guidelines can help you with future submissions.

Becoming known is more effectively accomplished through getting the free publicity mentioned in the above techniques. Why pay for something you can get free? When you get in the habit of looking at promotion this way, you will notice other 'free' possibilities as time goes by.

6) Paid advertising: Consider this story, however. A moderately successful artist I know of, was doing well with sales through brokers and galleries. One day he decided to hire a business manager. This person convinced him to start advertising his work in a magazine called *Southwest Art*. His ads consisted of photos of some of his works and his studio address. People began to call. One piece in the ad was sold to a reader for $10,000. After some months of increased interest in his work, the artist took his work out of the galleries and enlarged his home studio to include a showroom. He told me that even with paying high prices for the ads, he was making 30 to 40% more than he cleared with gallery sales after they took their cut, and sales were increasing, and his name was getting better known.

7) Art brokers: Designers often have direct say-so in commissioning art-work for a corporation. For convenience, they often use brokers in searching for appropriate pieces. Art brokers are familiar with the corporate art purchase process and act as an agent in taking care of the business details.

Sometimes galleries also act as agents but may be limited in experience when it comes to commercial art commissions. A big advantage of having a representative is the relief of dealing with the legalities of contracts. A broker acts as liaison between you and the company, usually earning a percentage of the commission as a fee. Initially, brokers will ask you for a set of slides of your most recent work, a photo portfolio, a vitae or resume, and a list of which of the pieces are available for sale.

A friend of mine who admired some of my wall hangings, told me several times that I should get in touch with his brother-in-law about selling my woven rugs. Maybe I had wax in my ears or something, because despite his repeated insistence, I didn't seem to get the message. But months later, while I was in New York City, I met the friend again and this time I heard his words, *"Call my brother-in-law. He lives just outside New York. He's a super nice guy. He buys the art for IBM."*

HE BUYS THE ART FOR IBM!   Why didn't you say so?

When I called the man, he was indeed, very nice. Unfortunately, he had just retired. But, he gave me the names of two of the brokerage services he used frequently while at IBM. Upon contacting them, they asked for 20 slides of my work and prices that allowed for 33% commission to them as brokers.

Sources of corporate purchasers

Listings of companies, public agencies and art consultants/brokers that buy are act as agents for fiber art are found from the following:

- Your state art council or the National Assembly of State Arts Agencies publishes information about public art opportunities and other books. Write them at 1010 Vermont Ave. NW, Suite 920, Washington, DC 20005, (202) 347-6352.

- *Money for Visual Artists: A Comprehensive Resource Guide* edited by Suzanne Niemwyer, information in the Bookshelf at the end of this book.

- *ArtNetwork,* 13284 Rices Crossing Rd., Renaissance, CA 95962 (800) 383-0677. Over 30 different mailing lists of artworld professionals including architects, designers, design centers, corporations collecting art, and many more. Average price of each list is $65 per 1,000 names.

- *The Guild: The Architect's Source of Artists and Artisans* lists art consultants and representatives and more. Available from Kraus Sikes, 228 State St., Madison, WI 53703, (800) 969 1556.

● Unique Programs, PO Box 9910, Marina del Rey, CA 90295. Their lists include over 1,000 galleries, 240 competitions, 260 museums and universities, 188 art publishers, 320 corporate collectors, 710 interior designers, 750 architects, 100 department stores and hotels. List prices range from $27 to $45 each.

● *ARTnews International Directory of Corporate Art Collections* (sells list) from Business Committee for the Arts, 1775 Broadway, NY, NY 10019.

Also, museums, state art councils and organizations like those listed on page 92 maintain slide libraries, open to view by purchasers, where you can place slides of your work.

How to seek commissions

By using the techniques mentioned above, you put your name and work in the art market to such an extent that brokers, design firms, architects, gallery owners and others know who you are, where you are and what you do. You can personally call on prospective clients or send letters of introduction along with your resume and photos. Usually, a corporation or organization will have someone in charge of art acquisitions like my friend in New York. This person will often be the public relations director, but could be in the design and planning area.

In any meeting, your past reviews, portfolio or models of previous works will tell the purchaser what they can expect from you. Let them know, in a professional way, what you do and how to contact you when they seek bids on commissioned work. A broker will most likely only present you to their established clients after being assured you can complete the project. Creative ability is only part of what corporate purchasers are looking for. They also want a team player, someone with the ability to work as part of a project group involving designers, architects, engineers and management. Purchasers invest in the artist's future success, as much as the work they buy today.

Sizing up the job

Suppose you're commissioned to do a new piece that is not a purchase of an existing work. It's easy to get carried away with the excitement of becoming a recognized and paid artist, but can you do the job? Here are the details you must be capable of handling:

● There is always a deadline for completion of the work. How closely can you estimate your work time required? Don't be afraid to increase your first estimate. If something can go wrong, it will.

- Do you have experience in all the skills you need to finish the project, including an understanding of structural needs? If not, can you learn the techniques and materials in the time allowed?

- Will the fibers require flame retardance? How will the colors of the materials be affected by light? How should the piece be maintained through the years? Will the woven art get natural or artificial lighting?

- What are the colors of the room; walls, floors, ceiling? Can you work with the project directions of someone who may have artistic senses different from your own?

- From where in the room will the piece be most often viewed? Viewing distance will affect the finished size.

- What is the size of the piece? What is the size and shape of the room? What is the design of the architecture, furniture or materials present? Ask the designer for a copy of the blueprints for specifications.

After you know the basic project needs, you are ready to make your proposal. It should include drawings of your ideas, samples of the materials and fibers you will use, and possibly a scaled-down model of the piece.

Pricing the art piece

Market value of art work is affected by the reputation of the artist and the state of the general economy. As you grow in experience and reputation, your work's market value also grows. All fiber art is not created equal.

Disregarding the artist's reputation for the moment, traditional tapestry should be priced higher than woven sculptured pieces on a 'per foot' basis. You must also consider the cost of a variety of materials like papers, fibers, cane, metallics, or many others. Size of the work and cost of structural support need to be calculated, too. When quoting prices on a bid, you need a point of reference that accurately reflects your cost of production. Chapter 2 can tell you how to figure the yearly amount it costs you to do business. Operating expenses or indirect costs will be similar whether you weave scarves, earrings or 20 ft. tapestries. If you know you can weave a square foot of tapestry fabric in three hours, you can calculate your 'per foot cost' the way shown earlier. Production cost is the sum of your indirect costs, labor and materials costs. Yarn costs can be calculated by weighing the entire piece, plus any warp ends or cut away yarns used in the production but not part of the finished work.

Don't be surprised if the price you come up with is $100 to $200 per square foot or more. This is not too high for corporate art. In fact, it may be too low. Fiber art works increase in value according to the success of the artist.

If you are working through a broker, the commission you pay them should be added to the total price. There is a simple formula for adding the broker's percentage that leaves you the required amount. Say that you want $4,000 for a piece and the agent will receive 33% as commission. You need to find the total amount that subtracting 33% from will leave you with $4,000. Divide the $4,000 by the reciprocal of the percentage going to the agent (100% - 33% = 67%, or .67). $4,000 divided by .67 = $5,970. To check it, simply subtract 33% (.33) of $5,970. This gives you $1,970 for the agent and $4,000 for you. Wheh!

Draw up a contract covering the details of fees after you have been awarded a commission. See more on contracts near the end of this chapter. Make sure you have added in the time you spent creating a model or sample, meetings with the designers, delivery and installation costs, and agent commissions. You should receive half the fee in advance to purchase the yarns and materials needed. Balance of payment will be due on completion and installation.

Work/study opportunities

If you want to weave fiber art but have no experience, consider apprenticing with an artist or studio, whose style of work you admire. This is the best way to gain first-hand working knowledge of how fiber art pieces are produced, marketed and installed. There are many outstanding weaving studios that produce commissioned work of large pieces. To learn of these opportunities, look through the classifieds of current issues of the weaving periodicals like *Fiberarts, Surface Design Journal* and *The Crafts Report*. They also have interviews and feature articles about successful fiber artists and the kind of work they do. Call the artist and explain your position; this is a good way to get a job doing what you like to do best.

Other sources of openings for fiber artists may be found in: *National Directory of Arts Internships* available from American Council for the Arts ($35 plus $4 shipping). *The Crafts Report* and *The Surface Design Journal* often print notices of available positions in large studios. Also try the *National Arts Placement Newsletter*, 1916 Association Dr., Reston, VA 22091 (703) 860-8000. They offer listings of studio artist job openings.

Selling to the interior design market

Interiors may be the most lucrative market for a handweaver as well as other crafts. Billions of dollars are spent on construction and remodeling every year. Avenues to this huge industry are opened through interior decorators, architects and interior design trade shows. A large variety of handwoven products are suitable for the interiors trade including tapestries, wall hangings, room dividers or screens, fabric by the yard, sample pieces or strike-offs, rugs for office and homes, pillows, throws, passamentaries and trims, woven fiber sculpture and more.

Styles are always changing, providing new opportunities and design challenges for the handweaver. *Metropolitan Home* magazine explores craft designs for the home. Other magazines like *Architectural Digest* and *Better Homes and Gardens* also show trends and can be a source of product ideas.

With the mark-up that a decorator charges their customer, the potential income for a weaver is good. A showroom for an interior design firm may buy pieces outright or typically charge around 25% commission on sales of interior fabrics. You can expect to make more money "per yard" on your weaving in this area than in making and selling woven products direct to consumers through craft shows or stores. This is because most consumers who use the services of an interior decorator have more money to spend.

In a wealthy location, you can get higher prices for the same piece that sells for less in a more moderate income level area. A friend of mine who learned to weave at the same time as I, stopped weaving to work in her sister and brother-in-law's yacht business in Florida. Eventually, she became the designer for the yachts' interiors. In this job, she purchases interior fabrics and furnishings from large design studio centers. She told me a handwoven throw about 40" by 72" was purchased from the design center for around $400. Quality of the throw's material was below the level of fabric we were weaving in New Mexico. For a similar size piece of much better work, we were getting less than $200 retail. I think we missed the boat . . . I mean the yacht.

Local designers

Look at what your market is by visiting local interiors stores, home shows and open houses, when advertised. You can get a feel for whether you want to work with the style. You can locate names of interior decorators and retail outlets in the Yellow Pages. To set up an appointment, go by a showroom or make an introductory call and try to arrange a meeting with the designer to show your portfolio and leave photos or fabric samples. It will help you to keep track of your meetings by building a reference file of every potential customer, including information on the size and kind of business they do.

The first few times you approach a designer or architect, you may feel intimidated by the plush furnishings and elegant surroundings. The more meetings and presentations you make, the more your confidence will grow. Simply walk in, meet the owner, and show them some samples of the work you do. Ask their opinions and what they look for in handwoven fabrics.

The most important fact to remember in approaching this market is *BE PROFESSIONAL!* Persons working in interiors have sophisticated customers who often spend thousands of dollars to acquire a certain look for their home or office. Interior designers, however, like the advantages of working with local sources. Reliability is the big key here. To establish your credibility, prepare a portfolio of your previous work. Have samples of your fabrics that you can leave with them. You must also know the amount of fabric or products you are capable of producing and be ready to deliver the orders when you say you will.

You can find out what pieces in your area sell for by shopping an interior design showroom, most medium to large cities have several. Woven fabrics for interiors will require different fibers than those applied for clothing. For some products like upholstery fabric, materials have to meet industry standards for commercial use, sometimes including fire retardation.

Getting known in the interiors field

The best way to create demand for your work is to build a reputation with a lengthy record of achievements. You can also make use of the same promotional techniques used for the fiber artist.

Announcement

Carnegie Fabrics and the
American Craft Council
announce the Third
American Handweavers Competition.

The Competition is open to all weavers who are United States residents. Entries must be original and suitable for contract upholstery use. Designs previously produced commercially are not eligible.

Carnegie Fabrics will give awards ranging from $750 to $3,000 to the first five winners. Awards will be presented at the Merchandise Mart in Chicago during NEOCON 1992. Designs may also be considered for production by Carnegie under a purchase and royalty arrangement. Entries will be judged by a distinguished panel of interior designers.

Deadline   May 1, 1992

Entries must be received no later than May 1, 1992. The Competition prospectus and entry form can be obtained from:

Carnegie Fabrics, 110 North Centre Avenue
Rockville Centre, New York 11570
(516) 678-6770

Carnegie Fabrics and the American Craft Council believe that this Competition will create a new awareness in America's textile industry of the talent and potential of America's handweavers.

As in the art world, getting acclaim through winning competitions is an effective tool of self promotion. Fabric companies or trade organizations sponsor competitions for encouraging new work by textile artists. These contests offer awards of prize money and sometimes a 'royalties contract', like the one for most original textile designs for furniture upholstery sponsored by Carnegie Fabrics like the one shown on the previous page.

Contests are mentioned in the weaving and craft periodicals, *The Crafts Report,* and the publications of organizations mentioned in this chapter. Contest offices will send you an application and guidelines upon request.

Interior design organizations

Two large associations that can be useful in connecting with the interiors trade are the American Society of Interior Designers and the International Society of Interior Designers. If you can get yourself invited to one of their meetings, you will have the opportunity to meet those in the local interiors field, talk shop and probably receive some good leads. Check your Yellow Pages for members' listings under Interior Designers. Or, write to ASID, 608 Massachusetts Ave. NE, Washington, DC 20002-6006, and International Society of Interior Designers, 433 S. Spring St., Los Angeles, CA 90013. The national headquarters will have information on a branch office nearest you.

ASID Industry Foundation (IF) is a group of companies providing products and services to interior designers. IF publishes a member's directory in the May/June issue of the ASID Report. This directory lists current IF members, their representatives, and products. Advertising space is also available. Write to Industry Foundation, ASID at the above address or call (202) 546-3480.

Interior design trade shows

Interior design buyers can also be reached through regional and national trade shows. This is the best way to keep up with trends in colors, designs and living styles. Attend an interior's show to see what they are about and to get a view of what's currently happening in the market.

Largest of these shows is NEOCON, an exhibition of furnishings, accessories, textiles, wall and floor coverings and other products for interiors. The International Federation of Interior Architects/Designers World Congress exposition is held jointly with NEOCON in Chicago. For more information on these shows write NEOCON, Suite 470, The Merchandise Mart, 222 Merchandise Mart Plaza, Chicago, IL 60654, (312) 527-7600.

Wendy Rosen Agency, mentioned earlier in Chapter 6, sponsors exhibitions at the International Home Furnishings Market, aimed at the interiors trade, twice a year at High Point, North Carolina. High Point is considered the furniture center of the world, a good place for to gather ideas for trends in products.

Reweaving and restoration

Another avenue of income for the handweaver is repairing and restoring damaged tapestries and rugs to their original condition. Reweaving is a precise and demanding task that requires a background of extensive history on types of cultural motifs, looms, fibers and dyes. This is a science of intense detective work.

A friend of mine living in Santa Fe reweaves oriental and Navaho rugs. Of Iranian birth, She was educated in weaving restorations in Tehran. Different elements going into restoring a rug draw on her background as a weaver and dyer. She matches the dyes and yarns used hundreds of years ago so precisely, one cannot tell where the repairs took place. It seems the most tedious and time consuming part is replacing damaged warp threads. A large selection of yarns is kept on hand in order to match the original texture, spin and size.

Many museums and anthropologists attempt to maintain a textile artifact in its original condition to preserve the historical significance. But private owners and collectors often seek professional restoration for their damaged antique pieces. This includes furniture covering, curtains, and coverlets and rugs. Such precision commands a high price and a good reweaver is always busy. Apprenticing with a weaver doing this kind of work is the best way to get into the reweaving field.

Contracts

When working with the interiors trade, businesses that commission art, galleries or brokers, *always* make use of sales contracts and purchase orders. When you are represented by an agent in corporate commissions, part of their duties is to protect your interests via the proper legal agreements. If you have selected an established agent, they will have the experience with legalities to guide you through the contract process. This can save you money, time, and hassles. You will need a separate contract with them detailing the particulars of their fees and responsibilities. Whether you work with an agent or on your own, a contract should include specific terms like these:

● Description of the work and how the piece will be constructed.

- When the piece will be completed and delivered.

- How installation will be accomplished and by whom.

- Your fee for the work and when you will be paid.

- Possibility of differences in colors of yarns initially chosen due to variations in the dyes.

- Changes in the design or construction of the piece.

- Rights for reproduction.

- Ownership of models. You will want to keep them as examples of your work.

You may at some point consider using a lawyer with experience in legal areas that concern arts and crafts business. If you don't know one with this kind of background, write to Volunteer Lawyers for the Arts, 1 East 53rd Street, 6th Floor, New York, NY 10022, (212) 319-2787. They publish a directory of volunteer lawyers for the arts. Also, see the Bibliography for titles to help educate you on contracts, agreements and other legal issues; available from this publisher. Chapter 10 has more on legal advice and resources for craftspersons and artists.

Other artist resources

For more help on the business of art see *The Business of Being an Artist* by Daniel Grant, *How to Survive and Prosper as an Artist* by Carol Michels, *Supporting Yourself as an Artist* by Deborah Hoover, and *The Artist's Survival Manual* by Toby Klayman and Cobbett Steinberg.

Section 3

Plan To Succeed

Chapter 9   Production Tips for Saving Time and Money

There are many ways to speed up your production and cut costs. Time you save can be used to design new projects, or maybe take an extra day off. Tools and methods described here can save you hours, dollars and physical weariness.

Cutting costs of yarns

Cost of materials is one of the biggest expenses in any craft business. For a weaver, yarn is the one supply you can't do without. In planning for production weaving, there are a couple of tips to help keep your yarn bills down.

I found I could cut the cost of production by 30 to 40% when I used a lower cost yarn for warps and the fancier, more luxurious yarns for the weft. For example, I used a cotton warp with a mohair weft, resulting in a sturdy, rich looking fabric.

Use suppliers that offer credit terms of 30 days to pay for purchases. Most suppliers will extend you a month if you can come up with a couple of references. If you aren't already taking advantage of the 30 day terms, you're missing an excellent opportunity to forestall your costs.

Use a professional letterhead when approaching the major suppliers if you want to receive production weaver's discounts. Usually, some kind of discount is allowed for larger purchases.

Quantity orders appear to cost you more at the time, but you save by getting discounts on bulk orders. Also, shipping costs are lower per pound of yarn on larger orders. Price increases by the postal service and UPS make it imperative to save wherever you can.

Stock yarns

In production weaving, you often want to reorder yarns used for making consistent selling pieces. In these cases, you will pay more for the yarn because the supplier keeps it inventory, but you can continue to weave proven winners.

Use the sales report forms in Chapter 2 to keep track of what you're selling. With records of what colors and fibers sold, you can build your yarn inventory in a cost effective manner.

Look for sales, closeouts and mill ends

Yarn stores are great sources for bargains. You can often pick up yarns at prices below cost, because of sales and closeouts. In addition, several yarn suppliers specialize in providing mill ends and closeouts. Unless you are reproducing a line of products all exactly alike, you can save hundreds of dollars a year by using mill ends. What if you can't buy the yarn again? It only makes your inventory of finished pieces look more like a collection of one-of-a-kinds. This is a positive selling advantage for you.

Buy yarn that is inexpensive in cost, not cheap in quality. If the piece you weave disintegrates after the first or second washing because you used a flimsy yarn that was on sale, you not only did not save anything, you spent your valuable weaving time for nothing. You probably lost a customer, too.

Avoid 'collecting' yarn

If you don't have a good selection of colors, you can't create to your fullest capacity. But there's a fine line between buying yarn for production purposes and compulsive collecting.

It's often tempting to buy yarns you find irresistible but don't really need. Giving in to the temptation can doom you to tieing up your capital in excess yarn. I have abused my budget on yarn more often than I have over-spent on any other expense of doing business.

When you find you have yarns accumulating and not being used, take them to your weavers guild meetings. They often have yarn swaps where you can trade off your unwanted yarn for someone else's. Several times I have gotten with another weaver or two and put on a 'yarn garage sale'. Once, by calling all the weaving guild members and running an ad in the paper, we sold over $1,000 of yarn in one day.

Ten tips for speeding up production

1) Sectional warping saves you hours of tying up and standing and bending over a warping board or mill. It also eliminates knots and tangles that arise from trying to maintain even tension when dressing the loom with a long warp. My production time on longer warps, 1,000 inches or more, is cut by 30%.

When you find color combinations that sell consistently, it is more cost effective to make long warps of the same color fabric. You can wind on 3,000 inches or more of warp with even tension. By altering the wefts on a long warp, you can create enough variations that you don't die of boredom before you come to the end of your wind-on.

Sectional warping requires a sectional warp beam, a tension box, a multiple bobbin rack and lots of bobbins (cardboard are the cheapest). Cone racks can be bought or built that hold entire cones of yarn, cutting out the need to wind bobbins or spools.

A great help in keeping track of the number of turns you make for each section is a trip counter that counts rotations automatically. All of the supplies you need for converting most looms can be purchased from your loom manufacturer or a weaving equipment supplier like Robin & Russ Handweavers, 533 N. Adams St., McMinnville, OR 97128 or Earth Guild, 33 Haywood St., Asheville, NC 28801. Most of the major suppliers are listed in the appendix; write for their catalogs. I converted one of my looms to sectional warping for less than $200. When I figured out how much I saved, it was the best investment in equipment I ever made.

2) Use quick weaving combinations. Plain weave is one of the fastest weaves you can employ. Twills are also quick as are open loose weaves. Loose weaves also have better drape in garments.

Much of my production work is woven with one threading pattern, a complex twill variation that yields six or seven different patterns by altering the treadling sequence. This accomplishes a few good results. One, I don't have to spend much time tying up patterns. Two, treadling becomes an almost subconscious habit. And three, the patterns result in a consistency throughout my inventory.

3) Design your fabric in the warp. I learned from my weaving teacher to do most of my designing in the warp. This allows for quick one shuttle weaving in the weft.

4) Consider painting or dyeing warps, or finished garments. Weave in neutral colors, then paint or dye the fabric for dramatic effect. This way, a plainly woven material can be more quickly transformed into a gorgeous, one-of-a-kind art piece.

5) Sergers or overlock sewing machines. For a cleanly finished edge, nothing works as fast and neat as a serger. If you make clothing and you haven't used one of these machines yet, you'll be sold when you see what they can do. A serger gives you a clean edge and the ability to cut your fabric simultaneously. By first drawing your cut-outs on your fabric with chalk, you can then go on to cut and serge the edges.

Sergers come in three to five thread versions. Thread comes on big spools running anywhere from .50 on sale to $2 to $4 each. This means you need three or 4 spools of thread in any color. If you use your machine a lot, you will need several spools of threads for each color that you want on a seam.

There are several brands of sergers on the market. After looking at some brand new models, I bought one used from a sewing machine store for $400. Newer models cost from $700 to $2,000. Another source of used machines is the classified ads in your newspaper under 'Sewing Machines'. Also, watch the classifieds in *Threads, Handwoven, Weavers* and *Sew News.*

If you look at used machines, take some swatches of your woven fabric to test with. You want to see how secure the seam holds the woven fabric. Don't be afraid to push the serger's capacity. If it doesn't do the job, it isn't worth the money.

6) Rotary cutters. A rotary cutter resembles a pizza cutter. They cut through one or several layers of fabric with clean, fast accuracy. If you cut your own rags for rag rugs, you'll save yourself the blisters from constant use of scissors.

Another great advantage of a rotary cutter is the ability to cut the fabric on a flat surface without having to lift the material as when cutting with scissors. Your cuts are more accurate and you don't have as much unraveling from the handling process. It's a lot like cutting out cookie dough. Just line up the fabric and cut away.

7) Farm out the cutting and sewing. When you produce large amounts of fabric to make into garments or sewn products, consider hiring a seamstress or contracting the work to a production sewer. Hourly rates that most seamstresses charge is usually below the amount you pay yourself for weaving.

I taught myself to knit and sew because I could not afford to pay someone else to do it. After a year of doing all the finishing myself, I found I didn't have enough time to weave at the rate I wanted to expand my production.

One day I happened to walk by a sweater store that had extra cones of yarn for sale in the window. This store was a combination studio and retail outlet for a line of machine knitted sweaters and jackets. The owner was present the day I was there. I explained I was a production weaver and spending more time knitting and sewing than I wanted to. She asked me the dimensions of my knitted 'add-ons'. I gave her the size of my cuffs, waistbands and neckbands and she quickly quoted me a price for using her machine knitters to produce them. I was astounded to learn that what was taking me hours to accomplish could be had for about $15 in a matter of minutes.

A professional seamstress once expressed interest in some of my work. I made the remark that we should trade her sewing and finishing skills for my handwoven pieces. I never made a better deal. She cut, sewed and lined a length of specially woven fabric into an exquisite full length coat. She assessed her labor at $75, which was exactly the amount I was wholesaling a shawl she had been attracted to. I saved myself days of fidgeting and tedium; she received a handwoven shawl she could never have justified buying. This coat, after being admired for a few days by friends and other weavers, sold quickly for $400.

8) Electric bobbin winders. A labor saving device you may be using now is an electric bobbin winder. When you use large bobbins and long shuttles you save time because you wind fewer bobbins and when weaving, you have fewer ends to deal with.

9) Flying shuttles. Flying shuttles are small box kits that house shuttles that are passed back and forth through the shed by pulling a lever or rope. Some kits come with a four box flyshuttle to accommodate a variety of weft changes. Normally you must purchase a loom with a flyshuttle built on, though some manufacturers sell kits for their looms. They are most useful when your weaving width exceeds 48" to 54". On narrower looms, they don't pay off. With the wider warps like 60", you will find it almost impossible to weave without one.

10) Dobby system. A dobby head is a simple programming unit that is "programmed" by any weaver with basic pattern-drafting knowledge. Once the dobby is pegged up, it automatically controls the lifting sequence of multiple harnesses with the use of just two treadles. This allows weaving of fancy patterns that would be difficult on conventional looms. Weaving speed increases by as much as 8 to 10 times. You also don't make mistakes in the treadling, no matter how complicated the pattern.

Computers

As your business becomes bigger, you may think of purchasing a computer or a computer-assisted loom. Computer systems for you as a weaver can serve in at least three ways. First is in the area of design and production of your handwoven pieces. Second is in the keeping of business records like sales, customers' names and addresses and expenses. Third, you can log on to computer bulletin boards used by other textile workers and share information and software.

You could keep your business records by hand for the rest of your life and probably be quite content. But if you once experience the speed and convenience of using some of today's business computer programs, watch out, you might get hooked. A computer also helps you in financial and marketing planning by quickly producing reports that outline your business as a whole.

Computers seem terrifyingly complex to many. Yet, the computer has become 'personalized' in recent years, more user friendly. Also, prices drop monthly, making it financially easier to afford one. It may help you to know that the first computer was based on a working loom. Now, don't you feel better?

Basic computer facts

There are two terms you will often hear, hardware and software. Hardware is the physical components of a computer system; like the TV viewing screen, known as a monitor; the keyboard, much like a typewriter keyboard; a modem, which allows you to use phone lines for sending and receiving data; the printer; and the CPU or central processing unit that is the collective center for the electronic circuitry which runs the programs.

Programs and operating systems are part of the software. These are the instructions that carry out a multitude of calculations, graphic images and word processing tasks.

The vast amount of available software may seem overwhelming. Check with the resources mentioned later to help you evaluate your needs before you buy.

The personal computers market is currently divided among three major groups. There is the Macintosh or Mac, produced by Apple Computers.

There is the group of IBM personal computers, which includes many clones whose manufacturers have emulated IBM's designs and can mutually run the same software programs. And there is also Amiga computers, which has carved a market for itself in the world of video, animation and graphics. There are other systems, but the above are the most commonly known and referred to.

I learned on IBM systems and have found them adequate for my business and personal needs. I have heard it said though that MACs are more user friendly. Programs for weaving design and business applications are in abundant supply for either system. There are also conversion programs that let you take information and reports from one system and 'import' them to another. Recently, IBM and Apple Computers have come to agreements that will increase the compatibility of their systems.

Computer-assisted looms

At the time of this writing there are at least four or five manufacturers of computer-assisted loom systems. There are also numerous weaving design programs written by several software companies. There is a list of information for these sources in the Appendix.

AVL Looms is the most well known maker of computer-assisted loom systems. Their Compu-Dobby system links a personal computer with any AVL dobby loom. When used with an AVL Weaving Cartridge, the Compu-Dobby can be detached from the computer, freeing the computer for other uses and creating two workstations. For more information about AVL looms call 1(800)626-9615. Benefits of the AVL system include these:

- Compatible with Macintosh and the IBM family of computers.

- Optimizes efficiency by automatically controlling the lifting of any combination of harnesses.

- Increases productivity by allowing one to change designs at a computer keyboard or mouse.

- Automatically computes complex or lengthy twills.

- Allows the weaver to see designs on a monitor before they are woven into cloth.

- Produces drafts and allows changing of patterns quickly and easily.

- Stores or prints out a copy of hundreds of patterns without having to write them down.

- Weave with the equivalent of hundreds of treadles with no tie-up.

- Allows one to weave while someone else uses the computer for design or other purposes.

Define your needs

You can see from the above how a computer-assisted loom can aid in production and design of your handwoven fabrics. The ability to produce more work and create a larger variety of patterns increases your competitive advantages. Some considerations in terms of your business needs include: Are your orders growing faster than your current equipment's capacity to fill them? Do you want to expand your production to levels that allow you to sell to more markets? Would the use of the system produce enough additional profits that the system could pay for itself in a reasonable period? Is the cost of a computer-assisted loom system affordable at your current income level?

Because there is an abundance of computers and software packages to choose from, you may need help in making a selection. One way to start is to look at what the different software packages do and try to select the one(s) that will do the closest to what you want to accomplish. When you know what type of system uses the software you need, you can make the choice between IBM or MAC computers. You can read reviews of software programs in weaving magazines. You can also get information from software dealers and the resources listed below.

No one software package will do everything (yet). You'll probably want a program that creates drawdowns and controls the lifting of the shafts. Depending on the number of harnesses you have, you may want designing help for multi-harness patterns. Some better weaving programs on the market are Generation II, Patternland, Fiberworks PCW, SwiftWeave, ProWeave, Weave-It, and Mindweave.

For business purposes, you may want an accounting program like Quicken or Lotus 1-2-3. WordPerfect is the most popular of the word processing packages. If you have a long mailing list of contacts, you will need a data base program like DBase for keeping files of names, addresses and purchases that can be arranged, sorted and organized in report forms and labels in many different ways.

Shareware or public domain software

None of the software packages just mentioned are cheap. One way of acquiring low cost programs is to look at shareware or public domain software. Many of these programs will do the job for your accounting and word processing needs at a much lower cost than off-the-shelf software purchased in a computer store. These programs are usually available from $4 to $25 and can be ordered through catalogs giving descriptions of their function. Some sources are:

- PsL News, PO Box 35705, Houston, TX 77235-5705

- PC Software & Supply, Rte. 1, Box 219H, South Sioux City, NE 68776-9801

- Association of Shareware Professionals, 545 Grover Rd., Muskegon, MI 49442

- *Alfred Glossbrenner's Master Guide to Free Software for IBMs and Compatible Computers* by Alfred Glossbrenner.

Computer learning resources

Here are some resources specifically for weavers who use or want to learn to use computers.

- *Software for Weavers...A Resource*, Lois Larson, 25 Montcalm Ave., Camrose, Alberta T4V 2K9 Canada. A great resource book with extensive listing of software available to weavers.

- Computer Textile Exchange, PO Box 1065, Lafayette, CA, 94549. A newsletter for textile designers including reviews of software and hardware, plus tutorials and articles by weavers using computers. Published quarterly, $24 per year.

- Complex Weavers, Verda Elliott, 304 Spanish Oak Lane, Hendersonville, NC, 28739. Study groups include computers and weaving. Dues are $6.

- WeaveNet, Ravi Nielson, Maple Hill Software, Plainfield, VT 05667. Computer bulletin board system for weavers using Patternland. No fee, but you pay for the phone time if you call long distance to log on.

- Fibernet, Ron Parker, Rt.1, Box 153, Henning, MN 56551, phone: (218) 583-2419. Computer bulletin board for weavers and fiber artists accessed through a modem connected to your computer. Operates 24 hours, 7 days a week. Fibernet consists of messages from users and bulletins with useful information. There are software files that can be downloaded to your computer, including programs for weavers, knitters and other fiber enthusiasts. You will also find useful telecommunications packages.

- Boston Computer Society, 48 Grove St., Somerville, MA 02144 is a large computer users group that can help you locate a local users group if you can't find one. Many city newspapers list meeting times of local users clubs. You can pick up tips from going to one of their meetings. Many of these groups include beginners programs.

- Your library will have review sources of various systems. Also, see *InfoWorld* and *Consumer Reports*.

Where to buy computers

There is no shortage of stores with computers for sale. There are used computer stores in many major cities. You will also see ads in the newspapers by persons selling their computer system or printer because they are buying a newer model. Buying a used computer is not quite as risky as buying a used car. They usually work right or they don't work at all. The owner should allow you to run through some programs to check out the system.

Computer publications carry ads from suppliers and some mail order catalogs specialize in computer supply. One such catalog is J & R Music World, 59-50 Queens-Midtown Expressway, Maspeth, NY 11378-9896, (800) 221-8180. Another is Damark, 7101 Winnetka Ave. N., Minneapolis, MN 55429-0900, (800) 729-9000.

Development of personal computer systems is advancing at such a fast pace that the system you buy now will become outdated and cheaper in less than a year. There's no getting around this. Your best plan is to 1) define and list your needs, 2) check out before you buy, the current programs and hardware that come closest to your needs, 3) make sure that the software you want is compatible with the hardware and then 4) look for the best deal.

For a comprehensive, yet easy to read introduction to computers read *Computer Wimp No More* by John Bear, Ph.D.. This is one of the best manuals for computer beginners available.

Chapter 10   The Business of Business

When you set up of your business, there are basic legal requirements to follow. States and counties will differ as to the exact licenses and fees required, but the general procedure is similar. If you are working from home, you may be able to get by without some of these for awhile. Your home, however, may not be zoned for business operations. If you are quiet about what you are doing, no one may ever bother you. But, if an antagonistic neighbor or official gets wind of your activity, you could legally be shut down.

Permits and licenses

If your business operates under any name other than your own name, you must file for a fictitious name statement. This is also known as DBA or 'doing business as'. If you want to use a fictitious name for your business, apply at your county clerk's office. They will tell you the fees and application process. Part of the procedure is publishing your intention to use the name you plan to do business under in a local newspaper, usually for a period of two to four weeks.

You will also be required to get a local business license. This is a yearly permit to do business in the county or city where you will be operating. When you apply for the fictitious name statement, ask the county clerk for a business license application.

State sales tax

Most states levy a tax on products, and some services, sold in the state. You are required to collect and pay a tax on each sale that you make. Usually, the state sends you forms to fill out and return with payments monthly, quarterly or yearly.

Most states require a sales tax permit or resale number from every business that sells products. Sometimes the state will require a deposit from you as guarantee. You may convince them to grant you a temporary permit not requiring a deposit by presenting yourself as a part-time craftsperson doing only one or two shows. You can renew the permit if your business grows.

Apply at your state taxation and revenue office. As mentioned in Chapter 4, some craft show producers include the necessary information in their application procedure.

Federal identification number

For taxes, the federal government requires you use either your Social Security number or a Federal Employer Identification Number. If you do not have employees, you can use your Social Security number. Corporations and partnerships along with employers must get a federal identification number.

Legal forms of business

You must choose the legal form you wish to operate under. There are three legal forms that your business can take: 1) a sole proprietorship, 2) a partnership, or 3) a corporation or S-corporation.

Sole proprietorship

Sole proprietorship means that you are the sole owner. You own the business, manage the finances, pay the taxes and are responsible for the debts. Every business, including sole proprietors pay estimated income taxes four times a year.

In a sole proprietorship, you are personally responsible for the obligations of the business. In the event that damage claims are brought against your company, your personal assets, that is money and possessions, can be seized to satisfy them. Many small business owners incorporate their company to protect their personal property from this liability. Sole proprietorship is the easiest kind of business to set up and involves less paperwork than a partnership or corporation.

Partnership

A partnership means that two or more persons jointly own the business. Each partner is legally responsible for the financial debts and obligations of the partnership. This means that all partners can be held liable for actions taken by any other partner doing business under the company name. For example, if one partner borrowed money for the business, the other partners are personally responsible whether they knew about the loan or not. Lots of fun, yes?

Possible legal complications of a partnership business make the head spin.If one partner dies, their spouse may inherit that half of the business. Who makes the final decisions when conflicts arise? What happens if one partner wants to get out?

If you are considering a partnership with someone in a business, imagine that you are getting married to them. It takes the same hard work and compatible personalities to make either a success.

Corporation

A corporation is a business whose owner(s) are shareholders of the company's stock. The business is considered a separate entity from the owners, which means that owners, in general, are not personally liable for the debts and obligations of the corporation. There is also some measure of liability protection for the owners in lawsuits against the company.

A corporation's profits are double taxed. This means that the corporation pays income tax on year end profits and then when dividends are paid to the shareholders, they pay income tax on these profits again. There is more paper work involved with a corporation than other form of business.

Owner(s) can be hired as employees; that means their wages are an expense, deductible from the corporate income. Any other benefits given to the owner/ employee like insurance and paid vacations are also legitimate tax deductions.

Another form of corporation is called the S corporation. Its form is similar to the regular type except that the corporation itself does not pay income tax. Shareholders still pay tax on income from dividends.

Of the three forms of business mentioned, the sole proprietorship is the most suitable for you as a small business. If you open a retail store or your income from the business exceeds $25,000 a year, then incorporating might give you the advantages of liability protection and the tax deductions of your salary and benefits as a corporate expense.

When you have established yourself as a legal business, there are different systems you can use to keep track of where your money is going. The method you choose should be convenient and give you access to facts about your operation whenever you need them.

Recording inventory

Record your sales to an inventory record like the ones in Figure 10.0. This form is to track quantities of each item you make.
You should keep separate lists of 1) finished pieces, 2) yarns and other materials used in construction, and 3) all equipment used in your business,

Fig. 10.0 Product inventory record

Inventory Report for Item: Scarf

for Month: April   Quarter: II   Year: 1990

Date of Sale/Entry	Market	# of Items Made	# of Items Sold	What's Left
3/30				23
4/1		20		43
4/20	wholesale order		36	7
4/30		24		31

including looms, warping mills, sewing machines, shuttles, bobbins, and so on. There are several good reasons for doing this.

● An inventory of your finished, ready-to-sell goods is essential. By knowing how much stock you have, you can estimate the number of shows you can do and how many store orders you can fill. You can track sales of particular items, styles, colors, designs and contents to know what's selling and what's not.

Fig. 10.2 *Inventory and depreciation table for assets*

Assets/Equipment Inventory

Date of purch	Description of asset	Method of depr.	Write off period	Cost	Reduction for inv. credit	Write off	Balance to be depr.	Depr. 19__	Balance to be depr.	Depr. 19__	Balance to be depr.
10/86	loom		5 yr.	1,500		300	1,200	300	900	300	600

- Yarn and any other materials going into the production of a product is an expense deducted from the income of the sale, but only when the item is actually sold. Inventory of yarns, materials, and finished pieces not yet sold are all assets of your business, not deductible expenses.

- Equipment bought and used for your business can be depreciated over time, allowing you to deduct a percentage of the expense over a few years. Time periods and percentages change, so check with an accountant or tax guide book for more details. By keeping an inventory of your equipment purchases, including improvements and repairs, you will be in an excellent position to get the full amount of deductions allowed by the tax laws.

- Another excellent reason for keeping complete inventory records is to provide proof of value in the event you must make an insurance claim. Keep duplicates of your updated inventory records in a safe place like a safety deposit box at your bank.

Keeping records

Keeping inventory is just one of the essential recordkeeping habits you should adopt. If you set up an organized system for your records from the time you start business, you'll save countless hours of searching for important information and you can make instant decisions with the facts right in front of you.

As a business, you're legally required to keep records including receipts of sales. Receipts for expenditures provide proof of legal deductions from income for tax purposes. As a business, you are always subject to the possibility of a tax audit by the IRS. Prepare yourself. Follow a good record keeping plan and store your records safely. Keep all of your receipts for the last five years or longer. Beyond the legal requirements, it's inevitable that situations arise when you need to look up information from a previous year.

Keeping records is easy. Buy an inexpensive plastic file box from Wal-Mart or somewhere. Using file folders, set up files for your sales, each of your expense categories, bank statements, address lists, show applications and so on. Every time you buy something for business purposes, put the receipt in its proper file. Be sure to write on the receipt, if it isn't clear, what the expense was for. Your basic record keeping will come under these categories:

- A filing system such as the one just mentioned.

- Your business checkbook.

- Sales receipts and sales reports.

- Inventory listings of finished products, equipment, and raw materials

- Accounts payable and receivable. That is, money you owe and what's owed to you.

- General ledger for tracking daily transactions.

- Travel and entertainment expenses log. Keep a log like the example in Figure 10.3. Record the expenses and reason for the trip for all business related purposes.

Figure 10.3 Travel and entertainment expenses log

Travel and Entertainment Expenses Log				
Date	Location	Reason for expense	Client Information	Cost
3/15	Harvest Restaurant	Dinner	Mrs. Brown, store owner	38.50

Figure 10.4 Telephone log

Business Calls/Telephone Log						
Date	Time	Number called	Name of business called	Reason	Length of call	Billed amount
2/9/89	10AM	303-762-4958	Brown Gallery	set appointment	5 min.	4.38

You can track your business phone calls in the same manner. Make a log like the one in Figure 10.4 to record long distant phone calls by date, time and number for keeping track of expenses and to refer back to when needed.

Some of the other business expenses you are allowed to deduct include insurance, show rental fees, bank charges, trade periodicals, advertising, office supplies, utilities, contract labor, salaries, equipment rentals or repairs, depreciation, and the cost of goods sold. While on a business trip, save all motel and restaurant receipts, toll and parking fees.

IRS provides free publications outlining guidelines for taxpayers. Call (800) 424-3676 to order Publication 910 *Guide to Free Tax Services.* 910 lists all the publications you may need.

A sample expense log is on the following page in Figure 10.5. Workbooks for keeping track of expenses can be found at office supply stores and large bookstores. Two excellent guides to records keeping and operating a small business are *Small Time Operator* by Barnard Kamaroff and *Recordkeeping, The Secret to Growth and Profit* by Linda Pinson and Jerry Jinnett.

You may decide that figuring your taxes takes too much time. Ask other craftspersons and weavers which accountants they use. Try to locate a professional who has experience in arts and crafts businesses. For more information on getting low cost accounting advice, write to the Accountants for the Public Interest, 1012 14th St. NW, Suite 906, Washington, DC 20005. API is a national nonprofit organization whose purpose is to encourage accountants to volunteer their time and expertise to nonprofits, small businesses, and individuals who need low-cost professional accounting services. Work is carried out by a growing network of 19 affiliates and more than 4,000 volunteers across the country.

Figure 10.5 Expenses log

Expenses Log for: January											
Date	Check No.	Pay To	Amount	Rent	Utilities	Payroll	Advertising	Office Supplies	Postage	Taxes, License	Other
1/9	1132	ACE	$295	$295							
1/10	1133	Silver Co	$27					$27			
1/10	1134	US Post	$17						$17		

Insurance

At first, you may not want to add another monthly bill like insurance to the cost of staying in business. Insurance does give you a certain peace of mind though, if you have a large inventory of yarns, finished goods, and various pieces of equipment.

If you have children or dependents that would suffer financially from your having an accident, insurance coverage could save you and them hardship. You might need coverage for worker's compensation, fire, flood, theft and liability.

If you rent studio or business space, insurance may be required in the lease. If you work from home, it's your choice.

Employee injuries on the job can open you up to legal action. Employers are required in most states to provide worker's compensation insurance. This is an expense an employer cannot legally avoid.

If employees will be working from their own homes, workers compensation insurance rates will be more than twice the normal amount. They view home employees as high-risk. It would be easy for the worker at home all day to claim any injury as work related.

When you hire employees or contractors, adopt safety measures for all aspects of the work environment. For information on safety issues for craftspersons, write to *ACTS Facts*, the newsletter for Arts, Crafts and

Theater Safety at ACTS, 181 Thompson St., #23, New York, NY 10012, (212) 777-0062.

Some companies advertise that they handle crafts business insurance. Visual Artists Information Hotline 1-800-232-2789 will send you the names of artist organizations whose members are offered group and special insurance coverage. You can also sometimes find ads by insurance groups in periodicals like *The Crafts Report.*

When you have to file a claim, increase your chances of getting paid:

● Read the policy carefully. Make sure the policy and the insurance agent are clear about what will be covered.

● Be sure to inform the insurer of all equipment you use in your business.

● Notify your agent immediately when there is a loss.

● Make a thorough inventory of your equipment and products according to their costs. Save your receipts. Send a copy to the insurance agent. If you're inventories are large, take a videotape or photographs of everything covered and update whenever you purchase more.

If you travel a lot for shows and selling to stores, you should consider complete auto insurance coverage, including towing coverage as well. Membership in uuto clubs like AAA (American Automobile Association) or NMC (National Motor Club) offer a variety of benefits like towing, locksmith services, quickest route road maps and life insurance options. AAA usually has branch offices in major cities. Write to NMC at National Motor Club, 2711 Cedar Springs Rd., Dallas, TX 75201.

Employees

A one-person business is easier to manage than a shop with employees. When you hire workers, you spend much of your time preparing their work, training them in your techniques and correcting their mistakes. They won't do the quality of work you would. And the possibility is good that one day, a smart employee will take the knowledge they gained from working for you, plus some of your design ideas, and open a competing business.

Bureaucracy doesn't help the employer either. Our government has a mountain of paper work to add to your already crowded schedule. Whatever you pay a worker, figure in an additional 30% to cover the social security payments, unemployment insurance and worker's compensation insurance that employers must pay. Then add in the extra hours for accounting and record keeping to keep it all straight.

As sales grow, you may find yourself faced with the decision to use outside help. You become so busy that you need help to produce, design or cut and sew your products. You can avoid the extra paper work and payroll expenses of being an employer by hiring independent contractors. This means you pay them an hourly rate, flat fee per piece, or price per yard of woven fabric. They take care of their own tax withholding and worker's compensation insurance. Of the different payment methods you could arrange, it's better for you to pay for work by the piece, because you know clearly what your profit margin is in production costs.

The federal government has several criteria for deciding the status of workers on the job. If the contractor you use is performing their service to more than one business, has their own tools or equipment, is free to set their own hours and to hire their own assistants, and operating out of their own home or office, they will probably be looked upon as a legitimate contractor. If they work only for you and at your facility, the government considers them an employee. It is important that you identify the classification. IRS publishes *Circular E-Employer's Tax Guide,* a free set of legal guidelines and definitions.

Many businesses have been fined for hiring workers as contractors when the government later steps in and says they were really employees. IRS can assess you back payroll taxes that you had not counted on paying. This redefinition by the government is on the increase.

For businesses regularly using contract labor, consider the newsletter *The Independent Contractor Report.* It provides up-to-date information on legal cases and other topics about contractors. A free sample is available from *The Independent Contractor Report,* James Urquhart III Seminars, 2061 Business Center Dr., Suite 112, Irvine, CA 92715.

Another source of information on the legalities of contractor relationships is *Independent Contractor Contracts: Sample Provisions and Contractor Descriptions* published by Volunteer Lawyers for the Arts, 1991. To order, write Volunteer Lawyers for the Arts, Attn: Lynn Richardson, 1285 Avenue of the Americas, 3rd Fl., NY, NY 10019.

If the growth of your business requires hiring help, the biggest question in your mind probably should be whether you want to spend your time managing others, doing more paper work, or weaving and selling.

Raising money

How will you cover the costs of starting or expanding your business? If you have a loom, yarn and a place to weave, you have the necessities. But you will also need money for show rental fees, travel expenses, additional yarn to replace what you use, office supplies, photography, and production costs of promotional material like business cards, brochures and price lists.

After you are established, you'll see ways to build the business. You might want a computer-assisted loom that is faster and more effective for executing your design ideas. Increased sales could mean hiring someone to weave for you and larger and more frequent yarn purchases. You might want to do more shows and need capital for advance rental fees. These possibilities include only a few of the situations that arise in an expanding business.

Capital for your business could come from several different channels. Your own savings is the most likely source. Other possibilities are friends and relatives, personal credit cards, a business loan through your bank, a personal loan from your credit union, and grant funding from national, state or corporate programs.

Borrowing from friends or relatives

Friends might be willing to loan you money for your needs. Unless you are ready to risk their alienation if something goes wrong, it might be safer to ask them to co-sign a loan made through the bank. Your friend would still be liable if you fail to repay the loan. But if you are confident the opportunity for realizing greater profit is a good one, explain your plan in depth. Show them your business plan with all the actions you will take to increase sales and income to repay the loan. If you keep it on a business level, they will pick up on your confidence and your chances of getting their help and keeping their friendship improve.

Personal credit cards

There is probably no easier means of getting cash or make purchases than your own credit cards. With Mastercard, Visa or American Express, you can make cash advances at most banks for any amount of your available credit on the card. The money is available by your signature alone. Unfortunately, interest rates on credit cards are higher than almost any other lending source. If you don't repay the loans promptly, interest adds up quickly.

When you travel to make sales calls or to do craft shows, a credit card can handle most emergency repairs that come up with your car. You can also pay for motels and food without having to carry lots of cash. Again though, pay off the bills each statement or you'll find yourself owing more than you could possibly find is worth the convenience of having the cards.

If you don't have credit cards or a credit history, there are a couple of ways to get them. Your bank will issue you a card if you agree to assign your savings as collateral to the amount of your credit limit. In other words, they love to loan you your own money and charge you interest for using it. After some time has passed and you have proved you're a good credit risk, your collateral will be released.

Another method of acquiring cards is to apply first to the major oil companies like Shamrock, Exxon, Shell, Phillips 66 or others. Their requirements are less stringent and most of them will issue you a card quickly. Once you have established credit by making purchases and paying them off, then apply for the cards like Mastercard, Visa and American Express. You might also consider a long distance telephone credit card like AT&T, MCI or SPRINT for when you travel. If you have a home phone in your name, they are easy to get.

You're much more likely to get a credit card if you have a job or have an established source of income. So, if you are working now, get as much established credit as you can before embarking on your business.

Bank loans

Though credit cards are essentially bank loans, you can also apply directly to your bank for cash loans. Again, it is easier to get a loan once you have established credit by paying off previous loans. But even if you have, they will usually ask for collateral on a loan or a co-signer with good credit. Money lenders who review business loan applications of any kind will want to see a business plan. If you foresee seeking loans for your business, you will need to draft a detailed plan as described in the next chapter.

Financial institutions that make loans want confirmation that there is a demand for your handwoven products. This could be in the form of sales reports and letters from satisfied customers. Lenders care more about the marketability of your products than the product's novelty. They also want to know how the loan can generate enough extra business to pay back the money.

SBA

If your bank turns you down, another option is convincing the Small Business Administration (SBA) to back your loan. SBA does not usually make direct loans. It does guarantee from 75% to 90% of a loan, working through your bank. The SBA will not consider your application until you have been rejected by a bank.

As with the banks, you must convince them your plan will work. Show them your ideas in the form of a business plan and explain how you will carry them out. For a more detailed look at the process, see *SBA Loans; A Step by Step Guide* by Patrick D. O'Hara.

Beyond loaning money, your local SBA office is a great source for information on starting and running a business. They provide a series of how-to publications covering accounting, financing, pricing, management and many other topics.

Another help program usually found in the same offices as SBA is run by the Service Corps Of Retired Executives (SCORE). Here you will find retired executives who volunteer their experience in advising small new companies. They offer free and low-cost training in all the basics of running a business.

Small Business Institutes (SBI's) are sponsored through the SBA on over 500 university and college campuses. Management counseling is provided by students at senior or graduate levels in the business administration programs under faculty supervision.

Visit a SBA office near you to find out more about available assistance. Most major cities have a branch listed in the government pages of the phone book. Or call (800) 827-5722 for any information on the above services.

Credit unions

Credit unions are more friendly, assuming you are a member, but may not make you a business loan. Lending policies for members are less stringent than that of banks or savings and loans institutions. Credit unions are created to help the member/owners. You can become a member of one usually through association with a specific interest group like a co-op or as an employee of some field of education. When you seek a loan, say the money is for a vacation. Just don't take one, yet.

Other funding sources

Another source of funding a business can be through venture capitalists. For a percentage of ownership in the business, you can get money for financing from these companies. Such firms are listed in the books mentioned below. It's doubtful, however, that you would want to let someone else have a say in your business decisions, much less collect big portions of your profits. You probably want to maintain your independence as much as possible.

Grants are available for artists and craftspeople to develop their careers without the worry of paying bills. Sometimes the money given may be used to begin or expand the business end of an artist's work. See the funding sources listed in Chapter 8. In addition, books that list different money sources for businesses are:

- *Money For Visual Artists* edited by Suzanne Niemwyer

- *Free Money for Small Businesses & Entrepreneurs* by Laurie Blum

- *Government Giveaways for Entrepreneurs* by Matthew Lesko

- *Money Sources for Small Businesses* by William Allarid

Licensing your designs

Artists, including weavers, grant the rights to reproduce their works for specific markets and periods through licensing agreements. In exchange, the designer will receive a fee or a combination of fee plus royalties on sales.

In designing for the interiors trade, the potential income from licensing your unique patterns to major fabric companies is good. New York City is a fabric and design center. I came across several weavers' work that was beautiful and original enough to become licensed to large manufacturers.

A licensing agreement must cover many details of the artist/company arrangement. How will the royalties be determined? Will the designer receive a flat fee for the use of the design or an advance against future sales? Is the licensing agreement to cover a specific product usage or territory?

To find out more about how to negotiate a licensing agreement, read *Licensing Art and Design* by Caryn Leland. She shows how ideas and images can be turned into profitable business ventures through licensing. She also covers copyright, patent, and trademark laws; explanation of a licensing agreement; strategies for negotiation; example agreements for licensing, agents and the protection of ideas; and lists of trade shows and publications to help find manufacturers seeking designs.

Legal advice

You probably won't need legal services when you first start your business. After time though, situations will arise that require some forms of legal negotiation or documentation. One example is a contract between yourself and a business commissioning you for a project. Before you pay for an attorney's services, familiarize yourself with the information in the books listed below. If, afterwards you feel you are over your head in the complications, then consult an attorney. Check with Volunteer Lawyers for the Arts, 1 East 53rd Street, 6th Floor, NY, NY 10022. (212) 319-2787. They publish a directory of their members who volunteer or offer low cost legal advice for artists who cannot afford a lawyer. The following resources provide sample legal agreements of use to craftspersons:

- *Making it Legal: A Law Primer for Authors, Artists and Craftspeople* by Martha Blue gives some examples of contracts for artists in various situations. Ms. Blue is a weaver and a lawyer.

- *Business and Legal Forms for Fine Artists* by Tad Crawford

- *Legal Guide for the Visual Artist* by Tad Crawford

- *The Artist's Friendly Legal Guide* by North Light Books.

- *Business forms and Contracts in Plain English for Craftspeople* by Leonard DuBoff.

- *Legal Forms for the Designer* by Lee Epstein, introduction by Jack Lenor Larsen; weaver, designer and author.

See your library for more information.

Stay up-to-date

There are at least two excellent resources that offer news, advice, and reviews to help you keep up with marketing trends and changes in laws that affect home based businesses. *National Home Business Report,* Barbara Brabec, Editor, P.O. Box 2137, Naperville, IL 60565 is issued quarterly. *Home Income Reporter,* 15 Brunswick Lane, Wilmingboro, NJ 08046 is issued bimonthly. Every issue of both of these publications provides helpful tips that can save or make back much more than the cost of the subscription.

Chapter 11   Without A Plan, You Might As Well Be Playing Roulette

Why are you in business for yourself? You have hopes to gain financial independence, a greater sense of esteem, the freedom to spend your time as you will, and to find avenues that allow you to pursue creative endeavors. To achieve your needs, it's important that you have a clear picture of what your business is all about and to concentrate your energy and resources in effective actions. Four out of five small businesses fail within the first five years, usually because of a lack of planning or sufficient capital.

If your thoughts are vague about what you want, writing them down may clarify your thinking. Sometimes the things we really want are obscured by surface thoughts. Struggling to write will help you focus, organize and learn about what you want.

You'll probably resist the idea of preparing a plan because you think *"I have better things to do that are more important."* Without a focus, however, your production and marketing efforts tend to go any old which way, losing impact and costing you time and money.

When you start out and even as you expand, you are moving into territories you know little, or nothing about. Yet somehow, you need to find or make a road map of how to get there. Think of it in the same way you accomplish any weaving project. When you draft your weaving designs and patterns for a garment or product, you are making a plan for how you will produce the item. First, you have the idea. Then, you sketch it out and do a drawdown.

Next, you assemble your materials, or resources. Finally, you do the action of weaving and final assembly. A business plan can be thought of in the same way.

Many business guides advise creating a detailed plan of long term goals for the next three to five years. Realistically though, how do you know, when you're just starting, where you will be next year, much less in five? You may not need a multi-page comprehensive business plan until you approach a lender for borrowing money for business expansion.

A plan does not have to be elaborate, long term, permanent, restricting or tedious. It can be as simple as jotting down your notes and arranging them clearly. Simplest of business plans is an organized list of your ideas for how you will sell your products like in Figure 1.1 on page 18. The important thing is to get the thoughts down on paper. Keep them in a notebook or file folders. Divide them into topics like products to make, markets to sell to, promotional material and so on. Then list projects that should be attended to in the order of their importance. Using the information in previous chapters, you can draft an effective priorities schedule like the one presented later in this chapter.

Make planning and organizing a habit and you will accomplish more with your time. As your business grows, it becomes increasingly more difficult to remember important ideas that slip from memory. Without a plan, you find yourself attempting a hundred different tasks instead of focusing on the most important one in front of you.

A plan can be for next month, for 6 months or for two years or more. You can change it at any point. You can write it in simple words that say exactly what you mean. It's the focusing and organizing process, just as in the weaving, that is important. No, not just important, **ESSENTIAL!**

Change your plan whenever you get new information about markets, production methods, or your personal goals. You can believe changes *will* happen. Opportunities are found in every situation. Stay flexible and you'll increase the likelihood of prospering from the unexpected. A plan is a tool, not a religion. Experiences teach you more about your business as you go along.

Elements of a business plan

A comprehensive business plan is needed when you seek loans or credit extensions. Typically, a plan is divided into four or five sections including:

1) A title page with your company name, address, phone, trademark or logo, owners' names, date of the plan and the author.

2) Statement summarizing the purpose of your business. This can be two or three paragraphs telling briefly about your business, where it is located, how long you've been open, the reasons you are seeking a loan, how you will use the loan to bring in more business, how you intend to repay the loan and the size of your own financial investment.

3) A complete description of your business containing information on the products you produce, how they are made, cost of materials, labor and production, and how you reach your customers. You should also list your qualifications, employees, accounting methods, and insurance coverage. This part of your plan needs to show real figures.

4) Marketing plan that includes the different groups, like those mentioned in Chapter 1, who buy your products, how you reach them, how a loan will help you sell more products, how much and what kind of advertising you do, who is your competition, what makes your products unique, your previous experience and knowledge of weaving, and what the buying trends are in your product lines.

5) Financial statements that show your income needs, cash flow, budgets, profit and loss statements, break even point, and a financial summary of your business showing all of the just mentioned from the time you began doing business. You might also want to include copies of loan agreements, leases, references, equipment receipts, and business licenses.

An excellent guide to drafting a plan suitable to present to a bank or lender is *Anatomy of a Business Plan* by Linda Pinson and Jerry Jinnett. Included are several sample documents and do-it-yourself forms that every new business owner should know about.

You will want plans for your business that are user friendly. That is, plans that can be worked with easily and give you instant, first-hand information about where your business stands in any given area, at any given moment. To help in this process, think of yourself as three distinct persons, each with their own duties.

1) You are the production weaver; the designer and maker of the products you intend to sell. You schedule the time you want to spend working and possibly the hiring of outside help. To attain cost effective means of weaving you will need a production schedule of how much, how often and what kind of woven products you will make.

2) You are the marketing manager; you are responsible for finding ways to sell your work. You make the products you have to offer known to customers and why they should buy them from you. You evaluate previous sales efforts and plan for upcoming markets with a marketing plan that outlines who will want to buy your products, how and where you must go to reach these customers, and when or how often to reach them.

3) You are the financial and planning chief; you do the office work of keeping records, depositing incoming revenue, and paying bills and taxes. You will update bookkeeping records that tell you how much you need to operate your business on a daily, monthly or yearly basis, and where and when the money will come from.

It's good to evaluate your business at regular intervals, like once a month. What is the status of the business in each of the above areas? Are you pleased with the amount of work you are producing? Are you satisfied with sales? Are you making enough profit? How is the cash flowing? Is there more going out than coming in? Have you thought of new products, or new ways to sell more of the current inventory? Have you tried to sell new products to old customers?

Production schedule

If you're like many artisans, you work when you feel to, which is probably much of the time, but not always the same times every day. From recording a normal month's activity you should get a good idea of what you can comfortably produce. With such a schedule, you can then estimate the number of shows you can do and stores you can sell to. You can also calculate the exact amount of your labor costs. A production schedule might include the following divisions.

Part 1. How many of each item that you make do you currently produce in a month's time? What is the average number of hours it takes you to make each piece? A sample of a simplified work schedule would look something like this:

Items produced per month:		Total production time:	
Rag rugs =	12	for 1 36" x 60" rug =	2 hours
Place mats =	120	for 1 18" x 24" placemat =	.25 hour
Shawls =	20	for 1 28" x 70" shawl =	1.5 hours
Sweaters =	10	for 1 medium sz. sweater =	3.5 hours

Part 2. How many hours do you spend a month on sales and marketing? This includes the hours involved in doing a crafts show, making presentations or phone time talking to prospective customers, both wholesale and retail, and writing or designing promotional material. Example:

Hours at:	Jan.	Feb.	Mar.	April	May	Jun
Craft shows	0	12	35	12	65	24
Stores	2	0	3	2	6	7
Promotion material	4	2	0	0	0	3
Total	6	14	38	14	71	34

Part 3. How many hours do you spend per month doing office or paper work, including paying bills, ordering supplies, and evaluating your business? Example:

	Jan.	Feb.	Mar.	April	May	Jun
Office work hours:	12	15	10	24	16	10

Marketing plan

A marketing plan is a list items you make, the market groups that will buy these products, and the actions you will take to reach these markets. If you have just started selling, you won't have previous records to use in evaluating your market strategies. That's okay, just guess. It's the writing process that is important. Once you start making written outlines of what actions you will take, you are in a better position to carry out those plans.

Use the information in Chapter 1 to help you choose a line of handwoven products you think will sell. Define the different kinds of interest groups most likely to purchase these items. Then write down all of the different possible ways of getting your product in front of these potential buyers.

After your first year in business, you should have enough information to evaluate sales and profitability of all your products and markets. Maintain inventory records like those in Figure 10.0, page 121 and Figure 2.3, page 33 to see how each product does by market.

Transfer sales data from the sales report forms to the inventory records each month, quarter and year. Sales at craft shows and to wholesale accounts are easily tracked when you use report forms like the example of a Craft Show

Report shown in Figure 4.0, page 54. This form lists the sales, expenses and other important information about a craft show. You can also use it for mall shows, renaissance fairs and home boutiques. Every sale is listed with a description of its contents, color, and amount of the sale. You can find at a glance, all the details you need about how each item in your line is doing.

Sales from stores, galleries, sales reps, and catalogs can be recorded on the Wholesale Sales Reports in Figure 11.0. Again, there are places for content, color and sale amount. There is also an entry space for commissions so you can total the cost of using reps or agents when selling to wholesale accounts.

Your marketing plan really starts to work for you when you assign priorities to each activity that you plan for selling your products. By combining the data from Chapters 1 and 2 and the sales reports, you can learn where to focus your time, energy and resources to achieve maximum profits and cut potential losses. The more you know about your sales, the more accurate your calculations will be. You have enough information now to use a priorities worksheet. In Figure 11.1, consider every product's number of sales, market variables, profit, and ease of selling. Each entry is also allowed space for writing in actions. Here you can list the activities needed to increase or decrease a product's production, marketing, or pricing.

A marketing worksheet can be for any period of time you choose. But, it will be easier to do your record keeping on a consistent basis like monthly, quarterly and yearly. In the example, number of units sold, variables, profit and ease, each receive values according to the examples that follow.

Figure 11.0 Example of wholesale sales report

Wholesale and Miscellaneous Sales Report								
Month: August			Quarter: III			Year: 1990		
Account Name	Qty	Item	Fiber	Color	Price	Total Sales	Less Comm.	Net Sales
Brown Gallery	8	scarves	silk	pastel	$35	$280		$280
Unique Catalog	24	earrings	rayon & bead	earth tones	$27	$648		$648

● **Units sold.** Enter the number of pieces of this product sold for the period of time the worksheet covers.

● **Variables.** In Chapter 1, we looked at the various elements affecting a product's sales. Assign a value for each influence that furthers an item's potential sales. For instance: a product that will sell in all four seasons of the year will receive 4 points, one that will sell both wholesale and retail will receive two points, and so on.

> *Item's function:* Assign a value from 1 to 5. If a product is useful to more than one market group, it receives a higher value. For instance, a handwoven throw will be sought by consumers for the home market and interiors trade getting a value of two. Wall hangings will be purchased by home owners, interiors buyers, offices, and churches.

> *Geographic location:* Divide the country into regions, like Northeast, Southeast, South, Northwest, West, Midwest and Southwest. For each area that your product will sell in, give one point.

> *Demographics:* For every element such as age, sex, family style, occupation, income or religion, assign one point. For instance, if you make handwoven earrings, your customers will be women, all ages, most family styles, religions, and occupations; give 5 points here.

Fig. 11.1 Priorities worksheet

Marketing Priorities Worksheet				For Month September Quarter III Year 1990			
Product	**Market**	**Units Sold**	**Influential Variables**	**Item Profit**	**Ease of Selling**	**Total Points**	**Actions**
rag rug	craft shows	17	16	8	9	50	do more craft shows
pillow	craft shows	2	10	4	4	20	cut production in half; keep for diversity

Seasons: Each of the seasons spring, summer, fall and winter get one point. An item selling all year round will get 4 points.

Wholesale/retail: If an item will only be sold to stores, it gets one point, if you sell in both areas assign a value of two.

- **Profit:** Use the information in Chapter 2 to learn the profit gained from any item. Assign numbers 1 to 10, giving the highest profit items '10'.

- **Ease of selling:** This one is pure ease and enjoyment of the sales process; again using a scale of 1 to 10, with 10 the most pleasing.

When you have assigned number values to each product, add them up. Projects that will make the best use of your time, money and energy will generally be those with the highest totals.

Whenever you introduce a new product, enter as much of the above information that you have about it. You can now know what to do with each item that you make. The obvious choices will be to increase production on pieces that result in higher profits in the markets that are performing best and cut production of work and markets that aren't selling.

Organize, then ACT

Write down your marketing plans for each product you make. You now have priorities to help you do the tasks most important to the success of your business. All of the information presented so far has been to help you organize as much data as you can about your handwoven products. If you don't organize, you're chances of success become just that, chances, and statistics say not very good chances either. Once you know the big picture of products, costs, and markets, the next step is to act. All the planning in the world won't mean anything, if you don't put it into action. And actions work best when they originate from intelligent, focused choices.

Section 4

Selling Yourself, Everybody Does It

Chapter 12   How to Use Promotional Material

Throughout your promotional material, maintain a consistency of your image, typestyles and colors. This means business cards, letterheads, envelopes, brochures, and flyers should use the same styles and color inks to make your name more memorable to the reader.

There are many printers that make business cards, color post cards, brochures and flyers at varying rates and quantities. You can find local printers listed in the Yellow Pages. Another resource is the *Directory of Book, Catalog and Magazine Printers* by John Kremer which lists over 780 printers nationwide and overseas of catalogs, brochures, books, postcards, stationery and more. Printers are indexed by equipment used, printing services, location, toll-free numbers, typesetters, stock recycled papers, design and artwork, 4-color printers and more. This guide also defines terms used in the printing business and tells you the best ways to work with printers to assure you get exactly what you want.

When you write or call a printer, ask them to send samples of their work. Get samples from five or six different companies before you make a choice. Often the same company will produce photo cards, business cards, brochures, flyers and catalogs. Compare them to know if what they produce is what you want. Shopping around before you order any kind of promo material can result in big savings. I have found inexplicable price differences, sometimes as much as $100 or more for the same printing.

Two companies with quality brochures and postcards at competitive prices are: MWM Dexter, 107 Washington, Aurora, MO 65605, (800) 641-3398 and Mitchell Graphics, 2230 E. Mitchell, Petoskey, MI 49770, (800) 841-6793.

Postcards

Postcards are an inexpensive means of promoting yourself that can take the form of the simple US Post card, printed on the back with your announcement, or a color photo post card produced by a print shop. A professionally done photo card can have your company name and address on the blank side. You can also use these as special sale notices or invitational notes.

If you choose to sell through art and craft shows, you don't need to advertise the event, because show promoters take care of that. A good promoter will have spent several thousand dollars on radio, TV, billboards and newspaper ads to draw in the crowds. What you should do, however, is send out invitational postcards to customers in a city where you are returning to do a show you have exhibited at in the past.

Business cards

For business cards, the expense of having 500 nicely done cards is reasonable, however, for local craft shows, you could easily make a neat hand-done card using card stock paper from a local office supply store, a rubber stamp and a set of ink pens. Make several different cards and save the designs you don't use for future ideas. Below is an attractive card my wife Dianne designed with the use of two rubber stamps. There is small expense in the self-made card and a card with an old-fashioned, hand done look is a sales plus, especially at craft shows.

A big advantage of making your own business card is you can change it to target your sales efforts if you see an opportunity for which your current card is inappropriate. For instance, you might want one card for craft show sales and another for store accounts. If you want to place your work in more than one store in the same area, use another card with a different company name to ensure no conflicts with your other accounts.

Contents:

Care:

McPherson/Dillehay
Handweavers

Many stores don't want your address or phone to appear on the work they buy from you; they fear the loss of sales when customers go to you directly. A solution is to print your address and phone information at the bottom of the card, then cut it off when attaching the cards to pieces for sales to stores.

When increased sales, it becomes more cost-effective to have cards printed. Five hundred business cards will last a year unless you give them out at shows. When you do craft shows, many persons come into your booth and ask for your card. Most of these persons collect cards as their way of leaving without buying anything. Why should you pay for this? Some craftspeople tell me they never give out cards at craft shows unless it is to a paying customer or a prospective wholesale buyer.

In my first two years of doing shows, I gave cards to everyone that asked. I had cards printed twice in quantities of 500, so I must have given nearly 1,000 cards. No sales came, no phone calls, no leads. Now, I only hand out cards to store owners who give me their card in exchange.

As an alternative to saying 'no' to a customer asking for a card, I tell them *"I'm sorry, I'm out, can I put your name on my mailing list and send you information when I will be doing another show here."* Persons who agree to do this qualify as prospects for your customer mailing list

Care labels

You should have a label sewn in every piece that tells the fiber contents, your name as manufacturer, country of origin, and how to care or cleaning instructions. This is a legal requirement for any textiles, fabric, wool, or clothing. For more exact federal guidelines on labeling and packaging, write the Federal Trade Commission, Washington, DC 20580.

Most label making companies have a line of care labels ready to sew in. They also make customized name and care tags from your designs. I ordered sew-in labels to match my business cards and letterheads. This helps build a consistent image easily remembered. See the appendix for suppliers.

Hang tags

Every piece you sell should have a hanging tag that gives details about your product, the way it is produced, and you, the artist. Your name should become synonymous with the excellent quality of what you make.

Increase the personal message of your promotional material by including a story about you, your materials, equipment, where you weave, or anything else of interest. Your personal narrative can be incorporated into all of your promotional material.

If you work in a location with historical significance, emphasize this in your story. Once at a craft show, a man who was admiring my work asked me if I would be interested in placing some of my pieces in his family's gallery. Introducing himself as Daniel Ortega, he told me he was the eighth generation weaver of the Chimayo weavers north of Santa Fe, New Mexico. What a great sales tool that is, but that's probably more history than most of us can come up with.

Education, grants, awards and foreign studies add to your credentials, too. Write about the techniques you use and the loom itself. Almost every aspect of what you do in handweaving is a part of one of the world's oldest traditions. For more ideas on hang tags, look at craft items displayed in galleries and stores.

Brochures

For sales to wholesale accounts, a carefully designed brochure is essential. Not only does the brochure remind the store owner or buyer about your weaving, it conveys the impression of professionalism and staying power. This is very important in getting sales at larger trade shows. If you weave items that will be marketed through direct mail, you will want to include a brochure whenever you do a mailing. A brochure promotes your work without your personal sales presentation.

Collect several catalogs and mail order ads with brochures that have products like yours. Lay them all out and look at them. What attracts you to one or another of these? This is an easy way to get ideas on how you will want yours to look.

Graphics designers recommend the following formula in designing flyers and brochures. One third of the page should be graphics or photo, one third should be informational text including a headline, and one-third, the ordering instructions.

In writing headlines, stress the benefits of your products. Emphasize what makes your weaving different or special. Your words will be more effective if you clearly state how the customer will gain by buying your product. For example: "Feel warm and cozy tonight with a _____ handwoven throw," "Light up your love life with a dress from_____," or "Impress your home buyer with rugs from_____."

Create a separate page for your price list and order form. Make it clear to the customer exactly what you want them to do, as "Order today, Send your check to: (your name)," or "Use your MasterCard for easy payment." Making a separate page an order form gives you the flexibility of using the same brochure for both retail and wholesale promotions. Include a blank order form with every order you ship.

If you do a large wholesale business, chances are you will be redoing the brochure regularly and it may be more cost effective to include prices on the brochure page. Your product line will probably change at least once a year. This means new photos and lay-out work. If you mail to 50 stores or more, you'll want something more than a hand done flyer. A well produced brochure becomes a statement of the size and image of your business.

For a beginner with few accounts, the cost of preparing and printing color brochures is not worth it. In a few hours and for much less expense, you can design and produce much of the necessary materials using a local copy shop to run off as many or as few as you need.

Be sure your sales material contains clear instructions on where and how to place an order. Recently, I was designing a catalog of books. Under pressure to get them distributed by a certain date, I hastily produced the material. On my way to the event where I would have distributed the material, an unexpected delay prevented me from making the deadline. Reconciled to the inevitable, I thought to take another look at the lay-out. Upon examining it, I found that in my haste, I had left out the name and address for customers to order from.

Promotional material can also take the form of packaging. The public buys the packaging of a product because it raises the value they perceive in an item. One successful weaver packages every scarf or shawl in an ornate box with full color photography background on all sides. Although, the weaving could easily stand on its own merits, selling it in a beautiful box makes it more attractive and the weaver can ask a higher price.

Photos of your work

Photos and slides can be used for getting into juried shows, in a brochure, catalog, or log book of your projects, to accompany feature articles about your work, and in a portfolio to make presentations when seeking commissions. Get the best photos of your weaving that you can afford. You are competing with other weavers as well as commercially woven products. You want pictures to show how clothing looks on a customer; how rugs look in a nicely furnished room or office; or how a man's scarf looks around his neck.

If one photographer can't give you that look, find another one. A customer sees and remembers the pictures. You won't save any money taking cheap shots.

Have photos taken of your best pieces, you at work on the loom, and head-shots of you. Make a photo file to use for any media or jurying needs. As mentioned before, you may need several sets of slides to apply for shows with simultaneous application deadlines.

When shooting for jury purposes, use a backdrop that is neutral or flat black. Your craft work should fill the picture as much as possible. Lighting and focus should eliminate shadows and give depth of field to the piece. Halogen lights give the most white of artificial lighting. Fluorescent lighting casts a bluish tint and incandescent casts a reddish tint.

A book that deals with the subject of jury slide standards is *Photographing Your Craftwork* by Steve Meltzer. Though the book does not give any explicit examples of woven items, much of the information will be useful if you intend to shoot your work or hire someone without craft photography experience. Another source of photography tips is *Photographing Your Artwork* by Russell Hart.

Learn about what juries look for so that you can provide guidelines for your photographer to produce the kind of pictures that will help get you accepted into shows. To find an experienced crafts' photographer, check the classifieds in *The Crafts Report*. Request samples of their previous work to compare to your own needs.

Creating a logbook

Another use for photos is a production logbook. A logbook will have a picture of each piece or style with details of material costs, production time, drafts, EPI, shrinkage, sewing or assembly and notes about the work. A log can save you design and lay-out time when you're planning your schedule. It can also remind you of previous works that should be in expanded production. See Figure 12.0 on the next page.

Design and lay-out help

An excellent guide to lay-out and design for non-professional graphic artists is *Looking Good In Print* by Roger Parker. Clear and easy to read, it gives valuable advice on design elements in flyers, business cards, brochures, newsletters and other formats.

Fig. 11.1 Photo log/journal example

Photo Log/Journal   Item: Date:

Photo or sketch:

Tie-up: Treadling:

Project Description:

Accessories:
EPI and Sleying:
Width in Reed:
Warp Ends:
Warp Length:
PPI:
Shrinkage: Total Project Hours:
Weaving Instructions: Total Cost of Materials:
                                   Sales Performance:
Finishing and Assembly: Notes:

Chapter 13   How to Make Sales Happen

Selling what you make can be as natural as the making of it. People see your work, they fall in love, they buy. Sometimes, though, you need to make a few simple efforts when a customer is hesitant or on the verge of walking away. Techniques presented in this chapter revolve around generating friendliness between you and your buyer.

Customers respect you because you are a craftsperson. They buy handcrafted work because of its novelty as much as utility, so you have a ready market for your products. An easy going approach to sales will give you better results and more personal satisfaction. No one likes insensitive salespersons who mechanically repeat their 'attack' without regard for the human being they are trying to persuade.

Recognition

Everyone likes to be recognized, it makes them feel valued. It's the key to getting them to like you. Often, customers buy from you because they feel warmly towards you just as much as the attractiveness of your products. The simplest form of recognition is to greet each customer, even if it is only with a simple "Hello."

Find out your customer's name. Address them by their first name as often as you can without being obvious about it. You can learn to remember your customer's names with this simple trick. Think of the silliest image you can involving the person that makes use of all the syllables in the name. For example, Joe Rockefellar: imagine Joe dressed in diapers, barely contained in a huge cradle, rocking. The more ridiculous the image, the more likely you will remember the name.

Listen to customers when they talk. Get interested in them. Sales pitches won't help when you aren't listening to what your customer is saying. There is an immense variety of ways you can talk to people by just staying in the moment. Be friendly. Relax and focus on the person. Giving real attention to customers will warm them up to you and what you are selling.

Easy openers

Opening a conversation with a stranger is tough for many. An easy way to start an exchange is to ask an innocuous question that does not require a 'yes' or 'no' response. Any topic will do, as long as it starts a conversation. Avoid using the same lines over and over again with different persons. Think of things at hand, like complimenting them on their jewelry or handbag, or whatever seems natural.

Once you have broken the ice, you can then lead the direction of talk by asking questions that must be answered with 'yes', as when you see a woman wearing an outfit in purples and greens, *"You wear purples and greens well, don't you?"* When you can get the customer to make 'yes' affirmations one after another, you're closing question "Can I wrap this up for you?" has a better chance of getting a 'yes' reply.

Ask for the sale

There are many ways to ask for the sale. Often, making the request can turn the hesitant buyer into a paying customer. Some different ways to do this are: *Can I write this up for you?; Can I wrap this one up for you?; Would you like to put this on your charge card?; How would you like to pay for this?; You'll never find another piece like this one; I think you'll be pleased with this; Let me take your order.*

The problem with asking a question is that you leave the customer the choice of saying 'no'. At times during your presentation, you will get better results by telling the person what to do. For instance, I have noticed that when I ask customers if they would like to try on a piece they've been looking at, half the time, they say *"no, then I might want it."* This leaves you in an awkward position. As a solution, do this. When you see someone attracted to a piece, pick it up, take it to them and say *"here, try this on. See how it looks in the mirror."* They rarely refuse and often end up buying. Once a person tries a piece on, you're more than halfway to making the sale.

Stay focused on your intention

Remember, your intention is to sell your work. A relaxed and free flowing exchange can build a good relationship with the customer, but when you are talking, it often happens that your conversation can ramble. Stay focused by remembering the desired result is that the customer makes a purchase. The more you talk, the greater your chances of saying the wrong thing. With a person you just met, you never know what that something will be. Keep it simple and relaxed and you'll do much better.

Stress the benefits of your product

In your sales efforts, remember that the customer buys products based on their needs, not yours. Put emphasis on the benefits of buying your item.

"This wool and mohair jacket is warm, and feels so cozy."

"These rag rugs are incredibly durable. They'll stand up to everyday use for years."

"When you wear this coat, all the men will fall in love with you . . . I just know they will."

Product knowledge

The more you know and are able to say about what goes into your workmanship, the more sales you will make. You increase the 'perceived value' the customer places on your product. It also gains you the customer's confidence.

Learn about the different fibers and dyes and their history. It's a fascinating story that will interest your customers. Do you know the story of silk and how it is made? How about the cotton plant? Did you know that most of the world's mohair is from Angora goats raised in Texas? Where do dyes come from? What is the history of weaving?

Make it easy for your customers to buy

Have all the materials you need to complete a sale nearby whenever you make a presentation to a store buyer or exhibit at a crafts show. You need a receipt book, brochures, business cards, price lists, and bags for packaging the sale. At shows, make the money changing as quick as possible, especially when you're booth is crowded. Spending too much time with one customer can cause others to leave in a huff.

Selling from a full display

Whenever you do an exhibition or show, have a full display of items for sale. It is a fact of good merchandising; you'll sell more from a full display than one that has empty places.

Have a variety of colors, don't rely strictly on your own taste. Listen to what your customers tell you about colors and watch your sales reports to see what's selling. A color that does well in a crafts show may not do well in store sales. Try new combinations of texture and color and keep tracking the results.

Promote yourself

Use the free publicity techniques mentioned earlier in Chapter 8. Find out the name of the newspaper life-style editors in cities where you will be doing shows. Send them an introductory cover letter, copies of previous articles about you, awards and speeches you have given, a press release and photos of you at the loom. If articles about you appear, make photocopies of them and mount them in small frames to hang in front of your display. This is the most visible place for posting your awards from past competitions and exhibitions. Buyers invest in you as a recognized artist as much as the work they purchase.

Your story is a powerful sales tool

Somewhere in the years of your life, you have acquired a story. You may have won a competition with your weaving. You might be the third generation weaver in your family. Your studio is in an abandoned mill that you have renovated. There are many possibilities.

We have all had experiences that someone will relate to. Learning how to make use of this relationship can increase your sales and management effectiveness. As a technique for selling, relating real experiences works. Customers can feel when you are coming from your heart. A story of your experiences is a thread that will connect you to your customers. In a world overflowing with hype and glitz, people miss the presence of the real thing.

The *Dale Carnegie Course on Public Speaking and Human Relations* emphasizes relating to people with the story of an experience that actually happened to you instead of using memorized sales lines. In addition, this course teaches other effective ways to communicate personally and professionally.

Don't apologize

No one likes a loser. It doesn't pay to excuse yourself for being alive, new in business, a weaver or inartistic. Avoid making comments as *"I'm sorry, I know my prices are a little high, but I just started."* Weaving is a profession and you are an expert. You put in many hours to make each piece. Your work is worth the price.

Prejudice

Prejudice and criticism are attitudes that customers sense from you. Negativity will lose you a customer every time. Avoid making put-down comments about other weavers. You'll have more success in everything if you avoid negatives in your speech altogether. Pre-judging someone can be a mistake as well. In Chapter 5, I related a story of how my wife and I talked a store owner into carrying our work. When I first looked at the woman, I thought, *"I can't do business with this person."* I was rejecting her on a personal level for no clear reasons. By not giving in to my silent prejudice, I was able to establish a new account that later sold some of our most expensive pieces. And as time went by, I found my first impressions were hasty and superfluous.

You may be tired, but don't show it

Craft and trade shows require long hours with scant relief. It's tempting to sit and relax at times, but most of your customers aren't concerned with how long you've been standing and talking. They will perceive an element of boredom from you if they come upon you sitting down. Outdoor craft show buyers are more forgiving in this, but wholesale trade buyers are often rushed and have no patience for exhibitors who aren't ready to help them immediately.

Sometimes, no matter what you do, your work just doesn't sell. Before you give up the notion of being in business, read the helpful tips for turning sales losers into winners in the next chapter.

Chapter 14   What To Do If Your Work Isn't Selling

What do you do if your work isn't selling? Get a job, right? Wrong! At least, not until you have analyzed your situation thoroughly. Before you give up, try some of the mehods for increasing a product's sales in this chapter. Begin by asking these questions:

- Are the markets, I am trying to sell to, receptive to my work? If not, where else would my products be in demand?

- Am I using the wrong colors, fibers or designs?

- Can I increase the "perceived value" of my work to make it more attractive?

- Are my prices too high, or too low?

Market receptivity

Often you will find pieces of your work selling well in stores and going nowhere at arts and crafts shows, and vice versa. Some items simply don't sell in every market, but this doesn't mean the product won't sell elsewhere, or that you should stop making it.

One fall season, I produced several different garments that I considered my most creative weaving. Without a doubt, these pieces were the best I had made in six years of weaving. I was so confident of the prospects for the new work, I signed up for more shows than usual. What a nasty shock I had when the buying public at the fairs overlooked every new piece. I was so discouraged, I was ready to quit weaving completely. I decided instead to show the work to some prospective store buyers. They loved the new weaving and took every one of the new pieces.

Before this time, my sales in stores had been minimal. Because of the reception of the new work, I approached more stores and opened several good accounts. I knew all along there was nothing wrong with my weaving. I simply had been unaware of the possibility that they were *too good* for the craft show customer. Not surprisingly, the pieces that always sold well at the craft shows impressed the store owners least.

Sometimes the craft shows you get into aren't good reflections of your work's saleabilty. Read as many different reviews of a fair as you can find and talk to recent exhibitors. Be discriminate when selecting which shows to do. Read the craft show guides listed in the appendix for review information. Show performances can change quickly from year to year. I once signed up for a show at the Astrodome in Houston put on by Harvest Festivals, a producer out of California. Their first year's promotional efforts had drawn huge crowds, including some of my own family. Since I had a chance to visit folks and a place to stay, I took the risk of doing their second year's show.

My sales for the three day weekend exceeded $3,000. The next year, I had a conflict and couldn't return, so I told another weaver about the show, and she was accepted. Her work was similar to mine, yet she only had sales around $2,000. This didn't seem that bad, so the following year, I thought about trying it again myself. I should have guessed something was wrong, when the show sales person called me before I even sent in an application. They said there weren't many spaces left, but because I was a previous exhibitor, I could still get in. I kept putting off the decision until a month before the show, which is usually too late to get in. But the sales person called me again to assure me I had a space if I wanted to come. They told me I could even pay at the time of the fair. By then, I knew something had happened. Either another show in town was scheduled for the same weekend, or the promoters just couldn't get enough craftspeople to sign up.

I don't know why, but I decided to do the show anyway. Sure enough, there were only half as many craft exhibitors as before. Crowds were thin and sales were bad. I barely pulled in $800 for the show with $400 in expenses. Again, there was nothing wrong with my work, I simply was in the wrong show at the wrong time.

Change your display

If the public is attending but not coming into your booth at craft shows, change your display. It may cost you money to buy better fixtures, but if no one is buying your pieces, you're wasting money to do the show anyway. Check out how other booths look, including other crafts, not just fiber artists.

The type of hangers you use to display clothing will change the appearance of a garment. When I first started doing craft shows, I went for the cheapest hangers I could find. I found some plastic hangers at six for $1 and thought this was great. By chance, someone going out of the clothing business gave me about twenty hangers with straight shoulders and swivel hooks to hang by.

Pieces hanging on the straight hangers looked more as it would on a human shoulder compared to the slanted cheap hangers. Swivel hooks also make it easier to hang items in different display positions. Customers find it easier to look through the racks, too. I found a local used fixture store that sold me more of the straight swivel hangers for about .25 each. I also bought a bundle of inexpensive no-slip foam envelopes to go on each hanger.

How color affects sales

If there is one determinant that will affect your success in selling your craft products more than any other element, it will be the colors you choose to work with. People buy color, they are moved by it. Sure, you will always find a market for 'natural' colored work, but without the diversity of a wide and luxurious selection of color combinations, you can't compete with the vast array of products vying for your customer's dollars.

For inspiration, look through magazines like *Ornament, Vogue, Metropolitan Home, Better Homes and Gardens* and *Architectural Digest*. Look at the sky, the earth, the grasses, the birds, the mountains, and don't forget the malls. Yes, that's right, the malls. If you want to see a spectrum of what the public buys, take a leisurely stroll through a mall and just let your eyes take in the colors of clothes, accessories, jewelry, art, furniture and household items. Keep focused on the tones and combinations of colors you see. If you don't go home with at least two or three ideas, you probably forgot the exercise because you became distracted and bought something.

Often at craft shows, a customer has entered my booth with a color card book showing the colors they are supposed to wear or a piece of fabric that matches furniture they wish to complement with a throw. These colors usually fit into one of four seasonal descriptions: fall, winter, spring or summer. Even if you aren't personally attracted to the idea of color charts, you should be aware of colors associated by season so you can match a person with an appropriate color. For more detailed information about personal color charts, read *Color Me Beautiful* by Carol Jackson.

Watch your customers as they look through your pieces. Make notes of which pieces are tried on more than others. If customers continually ask for certain colors, produce a few to see what happens. If they start to sell, make more. Build an inventory with a wide selection. There are millions of clothing styles and homes with as many different arrangements of furniture, architecture and interior hues.

With clothing, few people can wear all colors successfully. Teal may be one of the exceptions, and for me, teal colored garments tend to sell better than almost any others. Nevertheless, a variety of selection will make sales increase. Give the customer a choice, they love to shop.

Customers at craft shows buy handwovens as an investment in a 'collectible item'. For their dollars, they want a piece to suit their personal color preferences, home decor and wardrobe, not what's in vogue today and gone tomorrow. Store sales, on the other hand, typically follow the fashion trends.

A few years ago, I tried an experiment. Colors for the coming season were peach and lavender. In the past, I had good success with these colors used separately, so I thought it worth taking a chance to see if following the trends would make a difference. I made a long warp with about 70% peach tones, 25% shades of lavender and 5% neutral colors. I wove off four pieces, varying the wefts to include peach, coral, neutrals and even a light blue. Only one of the pieces sold at craft shows, so I put the rest in stores. Every one of the pieces sold in the time allotted as the color's seasonal trend.

To find out what's coming in color trends, look through fashion and interiors magazines. Gather mail order catalogs like *L.L. Bean, J. Crew, Eddie Bauer* and so on. They will give you ideas of color expected in garments and home decor, months ahead of the season. Remember though, you only have a couple of months to produce these colors and market them. By the time you are weaving with the same colors that show up in stores, the trend is on its way out. Colors for rugs and household items do not change as rapidly as those in fashion.

Several companies provide color forecasting services, but they are generally too expensive and impractical for a handweaver doing a small business. A more reasonable resource is *Color Trends*. This book comes out annually with photos and fabric swatches from unique fabrics around the world. It includes a variety of articles on color and a section on colors forecasted for the year ahead. You get information you can use and a beautifully created collector's edition. Ordering information about *Color Trends* is available from Color Trends, 8037 9th NW, Seattle, WA 98117.

By chance, my wife and I met a man who imported ancient textiles from Peru and South America. He acted as a broker to museums and private collectors for centuries old woven fabrics unearthed at archeological digs. I don't know how he got his hands on them. He showed me a few of the unmounted pieces he had that were dated at 2,000 and 3,000 years old. The woven patterns were impressive, but what struck me even more, was the colors the ancient weavers used. Despite the difference between natural dyes and the commercial dyes of industry, they were much like the rich earth tones and pastels popular today.

Certain color combinations I have used in my weaving have been good sellers for several years at craft shows. Some colors only seem to do well in stores. The stronger Latin colors like bright yellow, green, orange or violet aren't as popular in handwovens, possibly because they resemble the imported Guatemalan fabrics widely available at little cost. Yellow clothing doesn't seem to go over at all. For years, I showed a friend's beautifully piece woven in yellow as the major color. Workmanship was excellent, but show after show, year after year, no one bought it.

How content can improve sales

If you have trouble moving a particular item, consider weaving the same piece with a more expensive yarn fiber. Silk, angora, wool and mohair fibers are recognized as making higher quality fabric.

I was having good sales for two years with cotton shawls when, for no apparent reason, the public stopped buying them completely. I was hesitant to stop making a classic item, I changed the fiber content to mohair. The new shawls sold right away. I also increased the price, without a single complaint. I was convinced of the wisdom of the change when I easily sold the mohair shawls again in a city 900 miles away, with a warmer climate.

Try using alternative materials to add texture, glamour, and distinction to placemats, rugs and art pieces. For example, use braids, ribbons, reeds, leather strips, paper, fringes, and trimming from other fabrics like kimonos. Weave a small sample piece to see how these materials work.

Designing to sell

Saleable fabric design for clothing includes consideration of the finished garment before beginning to weave. What shape will the clothing take when worn? How will the fabric lay? Can the yarns used provide drape quality?

When you are weaving rugs, placemats or wall hangings, there are design principles that can improve attractiveness. A few of these elements include the fact that a rectangle is more attractive than a square, odd numbers create more interest than even, variety and diversity are more exciting than even spacing.

Proportion stripes using the Fibonacci Series; a number system in use since medieval times that contains design elements found frequently in nature. Every number in the series is found by adding the two numbers before. For example 1, 1, 2, 3, 5, 8, 13, 21 and so on. In designing piece with bands of different colors, stripes of one color could be woven 3", than another color 1", another 5", another 2", a 3" stripe and then two different 1" bands. For more on the subject of design elements, see the titles listed in the Bibliography.

Check your finishes

Finishing touches of your handwovens are extremely important to making sales. When I knew the bare minimum of sewing techniques, I ran into one store owner who literally picked my work to pieces, finding several flaws with my finishing. This was hard to take, because there was nothing wrong with the quality of the woven fabric. Fortunately though, I took it as the educational instruction it was meant as and focused on acquiring proper finishes.

Here are a few things to watch: With clothing and items like pillows, raw edges should be completely concealed. Check your fabric thoroughly for loose threads, skipped shots in the weaving and strength of seams. Use blind stitching whenever possible, to hide seams. Your cut edges should be finished with a serger or at least, a zig zag stitch. I found it easy to serge around the borders of the pieces of a garment after weaving and before washing and assembling.

Add fringe, decorative trim or additional woven bands of fabric to enhance the appearance of a piece. My wife, Dianne, took a plain weave sweater and then added trim from the cut-off warp ends and strung the yarns with assorted beads and baubles. This sweater that might have brought $100 in the pre-embellished state, sold at a price of $350 after the extra finishing. It sold so quickly, we could have gotten an even higher price and sold several more.

Finishing for rugs and placemats require limited or no sewing but cannot be ignored. There is any number of ways to tie off the fringes of your rugs to add that attractive detailed finish. See *The Techniques of Rug Weaving* and *Rug Weaving Techniques* by Peter Collingwood (Interweave Press).

Handwoven and *Shuttle Spindle & Dyepot* magazines feature articles providing advice for finishing touches. *Ornament* magazine has the latest and most original inspirations for wearable accessories and finishes. They also offer sources for locating unusually beautiful beads, baubles and other add-ons for clothing and jewelry. If you construct clothing or need new ideas for jewelry or rug fringes, these tips are invaluable. It wouldn't hurt to take a sewing class or two, either. Also see *Finishing Touches for the Handweaver* by Virginia West (Interweave Press, 1988) or *To the Finish* by Lura Bogdanor, 23 Cardigan Dr., St. Louis, MO 63135. More guides to finishing techniques can be found in the Bibliography.

Increasing the perceived value

Perceived value is the worth the customer places on a given purchase. If a piece isn't selling, you can increase its value in the eyes of the customer by various means. One way to do this is to make the item using more expensive materials and emphasize the expense and exclusiveness of the finished piece. Another way is to make use of hang tags, brochures and packaging to add value to a piece. It is unfortunately true that the public today often buys the 'packaging' of a product with the same regard for the contents. Though this may insult you as an artist, you might as well make use of the tendency.

Is the price too high, or too low?

You might think an item isn't selling because it's overpriced. There is a tendency among new artisans to mark down their products in an attempt to help the situation. This doesn't necessarily work. Unless you have tried and failed to move a piece for several months at a given price, you make a mistake in lowering the price thinking it will sell better. Typically, the opposite is more often true. I have often found that my work sold faster by raising the price, than by lowering it. This is because of the perceived value just mentioned. Sometimes the customer sees 'cheap' on a lower price tag and rejects the work as inferior.

However you price your pieces, quality of the work should justify the price you are asking. Any product should be designed and completed with attention to all the details. A finely planned and constructed piece will often sell better than a less attractive, less expensive piece regardless of the price, within reason.

Sales courses

Once you have done everything you can to improve the saleability of your work, there remains the possibility, slight though it may be, that you need some sales training. I have taken several courses in sales and even a survey course of methods specifically oriented to small businesses. I tend to use methods from all of them. It pays to know techniques, though not to use them blindly or mechanically. Often, I have made a sale to a customer who was wavering, by simply creating friendly conversation and getting them to linger in the booth long enough to try something on..

Chapter 13 contains many useful sales tips and bookstores and libraries will have no shortage of books on how to make sales. You can also find affordable sales classes at community colleges or continuing education programs of universities. The *Dale Carnegie Course* is a serious, but excellent investment, not just for your business, but for personal relationships, too. It is expensive, around $1,000, and the beauty of the course is, it works no matter what the level of your life experience is.

Section 5

This Is Not 'The End'

Chapter 15   Spin-Off Businesses

When you're in business for yourself, you meet and talk to hundreds of different persons over a short time. Often these conversations give you ideas about ways to expand your business. You begin to see financial opportunities related to your craft, even though they might lead away from the studio. In time, you may find yourself drawn full time in one of these other directions.

There are many different options available for income using the knowledge, experience and personal contacts you have gained from your weaving business. Here are some ideas that offer extra or alternative income. You could use them part time to supplement your income, but most of these spin-off businesses require as much, or more time as producing and selling hand-crafted products.

Teaching workshops

Teaching isn't limited to the famous; if you can do something, you can teach someone else. If you have no teaching experience, you can begin by reading some instructive books on basic techniques and get a picture of how training a student should progress.

Most colleges and universities have continuing education departments that offer many kinds of craft classes, including handweaving. Talk to the dean of continuing education to find out their teacher eligibility requirements. Teachers pay will be fixed, but guaranteed. Usually, you must apply for these kinds of teaching positions several months in advance, so plan far enough ahead to fit your production schedule.

You might also teach through a local yarn or craft supply store. Since the store already has a steady stream of customers, you don't have the advertising costs of trying to generate new students. Also, store owners will probably have an established class fee schedule of their own.

If you don't mind the public coming to your home or workplace, teaching from your studio gives you more freedom in setting up class times and controlling fees. You can advertise through putting up flyers at store bulletin boards, placing announcements in guild newsletters, weaving magazines, local classified papers and the 'community happenings' section of your newspaper. Announcements are free, ads cost money; both get your message out, so why pay?

When you announce your workshops, include all the information anyone could need to take the class like: what you are teaching, when and where the classes are held, who is the instructor and how much it costs.

It helps you to know how many students you will have. Include a request for advance registration with a deposit. Offering a slight discount for signing up ahead of time can induce more students to apply.

Charge the same for your workshops as others do for the same length classes, unless you offer expertise in some area of skill that is difficult to obtain. Then you can ask more for your time.

Generate a back-end business by selling supplies, books and equipment to students coming to your studio. A retail supply business quickly grows to involve more time than one person can handle and still find the hours to do full time craft production. If you have a spouse or a friend to mind the store, it's easier. I have come across many craftspeople who after starting a retail business no longer have any time left for their handcraft. Some end up selling the operation, preferring to return to making their craft.

Opening a retail craft store or gallery

Some handweavers and craftpersons open retail stores to sell their work direct to the public. They carry a large selection of weaving or complementary craftwork to help fill the shelves and displays.

Choosing the right location is the most important element for success in a retail venture. An area of a city that has a thriving tourist industry is an excellent choice. In a high traffic tourist area, customers are there to buy. You can see this by just hanging out for a day and watching. If you want a stronger criteria for deciding, you can predict a measure of your success by the number of similar businesses operating in the area.

Competition is not bad. In fact, if there is more than one business operating like the one you have in mind, it is a good sign. See *The Owner's and Manager's Market Analysis Workbook For Small to Moderate Retail and Service Establishments* by Wayne Lemmon. He gives helpful guidelines for estimating your market's possibilities through measuring your competitors.

Taking any location with cheap rent simply to get your business open can be disastrous. Inexpensive rent can't possibly make up for slow sales in a low traffic area. Also, recent reports suggest that sales of craft items in retail stores are rising while gallery sales of craft items are declining.

A friend of mine with no previous business experience, recently married a woman from his home town and they decided to open a consignment craft gallery. She had recently left a job with a similar type of gallery and had acquired some knowledge and enthusiasm for this kind of business.

They looked at several possible locations; one was a space that had become available in Old Town, Albuquerque. I was hoping they would take it, because they would be assured of a regular flow of tourist traffic, despite high rent; Old Town has many shops and galleries carrying handcrafted work.

Another location, the one they ended up taking, was in a small town 25 miles away. They chose a building there because the rent was cheap and the storefront was on a busy street near the downtown area. They also wanted to live in the low stress environment of a small town. When they first introduced me to the idea, their intent was to persuade other hand-crafters and myself to place our work in the store on consignment, which I did because they were friends.

They opened for business in early December, weeks later than planned due to unexpected delays and last minute changes. Pre-Christmas shopping was almost finished, but sales came in that would have, if continued month to month, kept them afloat. Unfortunately, they weren't aware that most retail store sales drop in January and February. Daily sales fell after the first of the year, far below the point of breaking even. Tension between them mounted and my friend had to take a night job to pay the store's bills.

Despite this, they managed to sell one of my pieces and sent a check. But when I deposited it, it came back "insufficient." After a few weeks and several phone calls, I finally received a money order. Later, I heard the store closed, and they left for other parts of the country. It was sad to see, but I hope I never forget the lesson of their example.

Not every retail venture is such a failure. A successful store can bring in huge profits over time. Many owners of going stores even open second and third outlets. *The Crafts Report* often includes feature articles about craftspersons who have retail success stories.

One retail survival trait is the owner's ability to provide exclusive merchandise to customers. Department stores trying to offer everything are losing business to shops that cater to specific niches in fashion and special interest.

If you intend to sell other crafts besides handwovens, you should educate yourself and your salespersons about the different media, how they are made, and the artisan's background. Hangtags with information as that described in Chapter 11 should be attached to every piece.

Before you open a store, list all the possible monthly expenses including getting a business license and fictitious name, signs, rental or lease deposits, first and last month rental payments at commercial rates, insurance against fire, theft and other loss, telephone at business rates, utilities, advertising, employees, inventory, fixtures and office supplies. Then add about 10%. Also, add in how much you will pay yourself, though you may hold off drawing a salary for a few months. If you have a spouse that can help with your other financial obligations, you are in a better position. Though perhaps, this is not the best reason for getting married.

You should plan to cover the operating expenses from your own pocket for the first year. If you can't, wait until you either have the money or can secure backing from friends or relatives. Most new businesses fail within the first five years because of inadequate capital and poor planning.

If you intend to open a gallery selling handcrafted work, take a lesson from other stores and get your inventory on consignment. It will cost you nothing but the bookkeeping and most craftspeople prefer to get their work in the stores than have it at home in a box. A cautionary word about this, however: Many times a craftsperson doing both show and store business will use their better inventory in the shows and 'dump the dogs' with consignment shops hoping the stores will do the work of selling them.

You can make your shop more appealing by making space for a loom or spinning wheel and either demonstrate weaving yourself or let a friend weave during store hours. If you sell other crafts, invite the artist to demonstrate as well. The public likes to learn what goes into the process. This allows them to see the amount of work in a piece and raises their perceived value of handmade products.

Consider all the details involved, especially choosing a location and having the capital to pay expenses until the business can support itself. *Small Store Success* by Ruth Pittman covers many basics of starting and running a retail store with insights from interviews with successful retailers. For trends in retail store operations, look periodicals like *Giftware News, Profitable Crafts Merchandising* and *Accessory Merchandising*.

If you feel you can work well with others, the federal government can offer you assistance in starting a co-op venture. *The Cooperative Approach to Crafts* by Jan Halkett, William Seymour, and Gerald Ely is available FREE from: U.S. Dept. of Agriculture, Agricultural Cooperative Service, Washington, DC 20250.

Producing craft shows

If you have done home parties with a couple of other craftspersons, you have the basic working knowledge needed to produce a craft show. It's easy to start with small, manageable events and then expand your operation to include more vendors, renting a larger space and doing more publicity to bring in bigger crowds.

There are many important details involved in producing a successful craft event. City permits are required. Advertising and publicity must be arranged well in advance. Craft exhibitors need to know far enough ahead of time to plan for the show, and there are countless other considerations like insurance, emergency procedures and extra help with organizing the event.

Pay-offs from producing craft shows can be good. Even a small, week-end event with 50 participants each paying $50 for a space will gross you $2,500, less your expenses. You may also want to set up your own booth in a prime location of the show. Two resources that give more detailed information on becoming a show promoter are:

● *How to Put On a Great Craft Show; First Time and Every Time* by Dianne and Lee Spiegel, from FairCraft Publishing, Box 5508, Mill Valley, CA 94942, (415) 924-3259

● *The Arts Festival Work Kit* by Pam Korza and Dian Magie, from Arts Extension Services, Div. of Continuing Education, University of Massachusetts, Amherst, MA 01003, (413) 545-2360.

Writing

Anyone can write about what they know. If you have ever experienced writer's block, writing about something close to you is the quickest solution.

Look through *Books In Print* in the library under the subject heading of weaving. A considerable volume of books has been published. The number of books about a given subject suggests the amount of interest the public has toward it and the potential market for sales.

If you're proficient in a technique or school of design, consider writing how-to articles for the weaving or craft magazines. Payment may be nominal, but as you become known as an expert, you will be sought out as a teacher and lecturer; for a fee, of course.

Becoming a sales rep

Many artisans prefer to work at home and and let someone else do the selling. For the person with a love of people, this provides an opportunity to represent several craftspersons' work, travel to different areas and meet with new store owners.

To build your business, attend craft shows and introduce yourself to exhibitors. Provide references and your fee and payment schedules. Run classified ads in the craft and weaving periodicals and *The Crafts Report*. Also, send your name and information to *Directory of Wholesale Reps for Craft Professionals*, Northwoods Trading Company, 13451 Essex Court, Eden Prairie, MN 55347. A listing here will bring responses from interested craft makers.

Use your computer to make money

If you own a computer that you use for design or for keeping track of business, you can also generate additional income by providing computer related services. There are scores of services you can offer but a few of them have the best potential for profit. Word processing and desktop publishing are probably the biggest markets. After you learn the software packages, you can operate a typing service, type books and manuscripts, transcribe legal and medical information, produce mailing lists, write letters, prepare business reports, resumes, newsletters and even provide technical and scientific word processing. One of the easiest ways to get started is to become a temporary overload service bureau for attorneys and doctors. You can learn the ropes of this kind of business by working for temporary agencies who send you on different assignments.

If you like programming, you might develop a software package that does something new and different. Marketing programs is similar to marketing your handwovens. Make a product the public wants, locate the groups that will have the most interest in buying, and focus your resources on selling to them.

Gaining proficiency with computers takes some time. Nevertheless, the learning curve moves swiftly upwards once you get interested. See Chapter 9 for learning about computer resources. Your library is a no-cost place to start your research.

For ideas on marketing computer services, read *Make Money Moonlighting* by John Mortz, *Word Processing Profits at Home, A Complete Business Plan* by Peggy Glenn, and *Desktop Publishing Success: How to Start and Run a Desktop Publishing Business* by Kramer and Lovaas. If these aren't available at your library, write to *The Whole Work Catalog*, PO Box 339, Boulder, CO 80306.

Chapter 16   Survival Tips

Twenty-three tips for surviving

Here are a few more helpful pointers. All of them have proven useful and many will save you time and hassles, not to mention, increase your profits.

1) Network

Networking is a great tool for anyone in a specialized field, especially the arts. Hooking in to a group that shares your interests opens doors to new opportunities. Many associations exist to help increase contacts, expand marketing efforts, provide information about funding, insurance, and legal advice. By joining or contacting one or more of these organizations, you can stay informed through newsletters and journals of timely events like legal issues, competitions, conventions and exhibitions. You also get the advantage of learning about other artists, designers and purchasers of art and craft work. Handweavers Guild of America is a national organization for weavers. They publish a quarterly magazine called *Shuttle Spindle & Dyepot,* an excellent resource for exhibitions, competitions, reviews and ideas for weaving projects. You may also find a local craft guild near you. These groups often do cooperative selling ventures for their members. For more information on how to make use of networks, see *Networking* by Jessica Lipnack & Jeffrey Stamps. Another resource is a newsletter for home-based mothers in business. Write to: *Connexions,* Box 1461, Manassas, VA 22110. ($3 for a sample issue).

2) Organize yourself

Get your ideas down on paper. Make frequent notes. Create files for ideas, receipts, customer addresses, and supplier information.

3) Stay informed about business

Books about business and marketing can help you gain insights to supplement your own experiences. Magazines and newsletters are a great source for production tips, supplier information, and fresh new ideas. See the Appendix for listings like *National Home Business Report* and *Home Income Reporter*.

4) Take classes

The more you know, the more you can do. Increase your technical skills and you gain competitive advantages in the marketplace. Yarn shops usually offer courses in weaving techniques. This is a good way to learn production methods such as sectional warping.

5) Work from home

Start making your products at home. Since you are already paying utilities, rent, or house payments, you won't increase your expenses and you can still spend time with your family.

6) Use what you got

Before you spend money for equipment and supplies, honestly assess whether you need them. See if you can't be more creative with yarns you haven't used for awhile. I took some three year old yarns, indisputably useless, and space-dyed them with great results.

7) Cut costs by sharing expenses

I share studio space with three other weavers. We all save on rent and utilities. Being a group, we also help generate enthusiasm for each one's work and business. We sometimes make large yarn orders together to receive bigger discounts. Sometimes we share booth space at craft shows. Cooperative selling makes it possible to do more shows.

8) Prepare for 'hot sales' times

Be ready for the good selling seasons, like the months before Christmas, with plenty of inventory. Once the season is past, it's several months before sales pick up. Use a production quota to insure you have the goods. Order your materials far enough ahead of the production time that you aren't ruined by out-of-stock problems with suppliers. Budget, so you'll have the money to buy what you need.

9) Establish credit with your suppliers

Most suppliers will grant 30 days terms to customers making frequent purchases. You'll be surprised what a difference having a month to pay your bills can make.

10) Get phone service in your own name

The phone company will charge you a higher rate for a business phone than for service in your name.

11) Save on travel expenses

If you look hard enough, you can always find ways to cut expenses. Lower your travel costs by doing shows in cities where you have friends and relatives. If you do many shows, chances are you will make good friends of other craftspeople. When your show schedules coincide, why not share motel costs?

12) Do your own building and maintenance

Cut down auto expenses. Learn how to do easy repairs on your car like changing your oil and tune-ups. Build, or find a friend to help you construct your display booths, inventory shelves or tables for your studio.

13) Make mistakes pay

Make your mistakes pay. If your project doesn't turn out for some reason, think of other ways to use what you've made.

14) Get payments for orders in advance

Whenever a customer wants something special made, ask for payment in advance. When a new wholesale account places an order, require them to pre-pay or accept the shipment C.O.D.

15) Get lean

You're beginning months will be the toughest. Sacrifice the fancy foods and pampering you could afford when you had a regular job. If you put your profits back into your business, it won't be long before you can afford to treat yourself whenever you feel.

16) Look at successful craft businesses for inspiration.

When I lived in New York City for a few months, I was looking for possible markets and weaving opportunities. I was surprised at the number of weavers doing big volume business. One weaver had two shops for displaying handwoven rep weave rugs that sold mostly to architects, designers, and interior decorators. Several weavers did large wholesale businesses weaving fine silk scarves. An owner of a couple of expensive retail clothing stores told me he was interested in buying handwoven fabric by the yard.

17) Contract the drudgery

If you don't like detail work, find a seamstress to do it for you. You can pay them by the hour or by the piece to do your cutting, sewing and finishing. This gives you more time to weave and design fabric.

18) Think BIG

You save time and increase your profits by "ganging up" your production. For example, if you weave rag rugs, wind on long lengths of the warp yarn. This cuts down production time per piece, increasing profits.

19) Avoid undercutting your store accounts

If you do a craft show in the same town where you have a store account, be sure to charge the same retail price that they are asking for similar products.

20) Use contracts

When working with galleries, designers or large exhibitions, draw up agreements clearly defining liability, how pieces will be shipped, who pays for the shipping, and who is in charge if something goes wrong. Clarifying these things in advance can save you hundreds, perhaps thousands of dollars in the event of confusion or unexpected misfortune.

21) Free and low cost help

Free advice can be obtained in many forms. Libraries provide books and references on every subject. Large organizations have toll free numbers and will send you free information. All you have to do is ask. For instance: Visual Artists Information Hotline (800) 232-2789; Small Business Administration national information (800) 827-5722; For information on getting low cost accounting advice, write to the Accountants for the Public Interest, 1012 14th St. NW, Suite 906, Washington, DC 20005.

22) Keep your eyes open for new opportunities

If you come across a store that sells handcrafted items, but not in your medium, approach them about carrying your work. Adding a new product line will increase sales for both of you.

23) Make extra income in slow times

If sales are slow or you just want to pick up some extra income, consider working for other production craftspersons. They often pay by the piece and you may be able to work at home. It may not be as creative as what you like, but it beats waiting tables or answering phones. Situations are found through ads in the craft periodicals, guild meetings, talking to exhibitors at crafts shows, bulletin boards at yarn or craft supply shops and listings with books on home business opportunities like *The Work-at-Home Sourcebook* from *The Whole Work Catalog,* 1515 23rd St., Boulder, CO 80306. $1.

If you happen to live in New York or New Jersey, there are many opportunities available through the New York State Employment Division. There are so many textile manufacturers headquartered in the New York City area, they have a special division for employment in the textile fields. Most of these openings involve jobs weaving sample pieces for fabric manufacturers.

Appendix A: Suppliers of Yarns, Looms, Equipment, Labels & Booth Displays

Alaska Rag Company
545 2nd Avenue
Fairbanks, Alaska 99701

Broadway Yarn Company
PO Box 1467
Sanford, NC 27331

Classic Elite Yarns
12 Perkins St.
Lowell, MA 01854

Cotton Clouds Mail Order Yarns
Rt 2, Desert Hills #16-WS
Safford, AZ 85546
(800)322-7888 In AZ:(602)428-7000

Crystal Palace
3006 San Pablo Ave.
Berkeley, CA 94702

Daft Dames Handcrafts
PO Box 148-S
Akron, NY 14001
(716) 542-4235

Earth Guild, Dept. WP
33 Haywood Street
Asheville, NC 28801
(800) 327-8448

Eaton Yarns
PO Box 665
Tarrytown, NY 10591

Edgemont Yarn Service, Inc. &
The Oriental Rug Co.
PO Box 205
Washington, KY 41096
(606) 759-7614

Fiesta Yarns
PO Box 2548
Corrales, NM 87048
(505) 897-4485

Frederick Fawcett
1304 Scott St.
Petaluma, CA 94954-1181

Ft. Crailo Yarns
PO Box G
Newburgh, NY 12550

GLAD RAGS
PO Box 237
Smithville, TX 78957

Grandor Yarns
716 E. Valley Pkwy
Escondido, CA 92025

Great Northern Weaving Supplies
PO Box 361
Augusta, MI 49012

Halcyon Yarn
12 School St.
Bath, ME 04530
1-800-341-0282 (US & Canada)
1-800-439-7909 (Maine)

Harrisville Designs
Main Street
Harrisville, NH 03450
(603) 827-3333

Henry's Attic
5 Mercury Avenue
Monroe, NY 10950
Tel. (914) 783-3930

J & H Clasgens Co.
2383 St., Rt. 132
New Richmond, OH 45157

JaggerSpun
PO Box 188 / Water St.
Springvale, ME 04083
(800) 225-8023 (207) 324-4455
Fax: (207) 490-2661

John Perkins
PO Box 8372
Greenville, SC 29604

Joseph Galler
27 W. 20th St.
New York, NY 10011

Old Mill Yarn
PO Box 8
Eaton Rapids, MI 48827

RAH Industries
801 E. 9th
Mountain Grove, MO 65711

Riverwalk Yarns
1912 River Rd
Burlington, NJ 08016

Robin & Russ
533 N. Adams St.
McMinnville, OR 97128

Roundup Wools
616 First St. West
Roundup, Mont. 59072

Schoolhouse Yarns
25495 SE Hoffmeister Rd
Boring, OR 97009

Silk City Fibers
155 Oxford St.
Paterson, NJ 07522

Treenway Crafts
725 Caledonia Ave
Victoria, BC, Canada V8T 1E4

Webs
PO Box 349
18 Kellogg Ave.
Amherst, MA 01004

WILDE YARNS
3737 Main Street
PO Box 4662, Dept. P
Philadelphia, PA 19127
(215) 482-8800

Yarns
PO Box 434
Uxbridge, MA 01569

Loom & Equipment Suppliers

AVL Looms
601 Orange St.
Chico, CA 95928

Gilmore Looms
1032 N. Broadway
Stockton, CA 95205

Glimakra Looms
1304 Scott St.
Petaluma, CA 94954

Harrisville Designs
Harrisville, NH 03450

J-Made Looms
PO Box 452
Oregon City, OR 97045
(503) 631-3973

Kessenich Looms
PO Box 4253
Greensboro, NC 27404

LeClerc Corp.
R.R. 1, Box 356-A
Champlain, NY 12919

Leesburg Looms & Supplies
113 W Van Buren St.
Leesburg, IN 46538
(219) 453-3554

Louet Sales
R.R. 4
Prescott, Ontario
Canada K0E 1T0

Macomber Looms
PO Box 186
York, ME 03909

Norwood Looms
Box 167
Fremont, MI 49412

Schact Spindle Co.
6101 Ben Place
Boulder, CO 80301

Label Suppliers

Alpha Impressions
4161 S. Main St.
Los Angeles, CA 90037

Charm Woven Labels
Box 30027
Portland, OR 97230

Heirloom Woven Labels
Grand Central Post Office
PO Box 2188
New York, NY 10163

Sterling Name Tape Co., Inc.
PO Box 1056
Winsted, CT 06098

Booth Display Suppliers

Canopies by Fred
9229 Sand Point Way NE
Seattle, WA 98115

Clark Manufacturing
339 E. Blaine St.
Corona, CA 91718-1303

Creative Energies
Rt. #4, Box 733
Silver Springs, FL 32688

Elaine Martin
Box 261
Highwood, IL 60040

Flourish Company
5763 Wheeler Rd.
Fayetteville, AR 72703

Hawaiian Sun
Box 5447
Louisville, KY 40205

John Mee Canopies
Box 11220
Birmingham, AL 35202

Quick & Easy, Mike Hutslar
1975 Holly Drive
Concord, CA 94520

Super Awning, Hazel Yoder
5 Town & Country Village, St. 545
San Jose, CA 95128

The Supply Source
8805 N. Main St.
Dayton, OH 45415

Appendix B: Organizations

Accountants for the Public Interest
1012 14th St. NW
Suite 906
Washington, DC 20005
(202) 347 1668

American Artists & Craftsmen Guild
PO Box 193
Westmont, IL 60559

American Council for the Arts
1285 Avenue of the Americas
3rd Floor
New York, NY 10019
(800) 321-4510

ACA Visual Artists Information Hotline
for funding sources, insurance, legal
questions, residencies, public art
programs, + other topics.
(800) 232-2789

American Craft Association
21 S. Eltings Corner Rd.
Highland, NY 12528
(800) 724-0859

American Craft Council
40 W. 53rd St.
New York, NY 10019
(212) 956 3535

American Crafts Retailers Assn.
Box 9
Woodstock, MD 21163

American Society of Interior Designers
608 Massachusetts Ave. NE
Washington, DC 20002-6006

American Tapestry Alliance
Rt. 1, Box 79-A
Goshen, VA 24439
(703) 997-5104

Arts Extension Service
Division of Continuing Education
University of Massachusetts
Amherst, MA 01003

The Artists Foundation
8 Park Plaza
Boston, MA 02116

Arts & Crafts Materials Institute
715 Boylston St.
Boston, MA 02116

The Crafts Center
1001 Connecticut Ave., NW
Washington D.C. 20036
(202) 728 9603

The Foundation Center
79 Fifth Ave.
NY, NY 10003
(800) 424-9836

Handweavers Guild of America
120 Mountain Ave., B101
Bloomfield, CT 06002
(203) 242 3577

Internal Revenue Service (IRS) provides
free publications outlining guidelines for
taxpayers. Call (800) 424-3676 to order
Publication 910 *Guide to Free Tax
Services.* 910 lists all the publications
you may need.

ITNET (International Tapestry Network)
PO Box 203228
Anchorage, AK 99520

National Assembly of
State Arts Agencies
1010 Vermont Ave. NW, Suite 920
Washington, DC 20005
(202) 347-6352

Nat'l Association of Arts & Crafts
5485 Beltline Rd., Suite 125
Dallas, TX 75240

National Association for the
Cottage Industry
PO Box 14850
Chicago, IL 60614
(312) 4728116

National Endowment for the Arts
1100 Pennsylvania Ave., NW
Room 710
Washington, DC 20506
(202) 682-5448

National Tabletop Association
355 Lexington Ave.
NY, NY 10017
(212) 661-4261

Ontario Crafts Council
35 McCaul St.
Toronto, Ontario M5T 1V7
Canada   (416) 977-3551

Professional Ass'n. of Custom Clothiers
1375 Broadway
NY, NY 10018
(212) 302-2150

Surface Design Association
PO Box 20799
Oakland, CA 94620

Volunteer Lawyers for the Arts
1 East 53rd Street, 6th Floor
New York, NY 10022
(212) 319-2787

Your local Weavers Guild

Your local SBA office

(Small Business Administration)
SCORE
(Service Core of Retired Executives)
SBIs
(Small Business Institutes)
If there is no office near you,
call (800) 827-5722 for information.

Check your state for state arts and
crafts councils or commissions or write
the National Assembly of State Arts
Agencies (listed on previous page)

Appendix C: Art & Craft Show Guides

Arts & Crafts Catalyst
PO Box 433
S. Whitley, IN 46787

Arts & Crafts Show Guide
208-D E. High St.
Jefferson City, MO 65101
(314) 636-0491

Craft Digest
PO Box 155
New Britain, CT 06050

Craft Show Bulletin
Box 1914
Westfield, MA 01086

Fairs & Festivals of the Southeast
Fairs & Festivals of the Northeast
Arts Extension Service
Division of Continuing Education
University of Massachusetts
Amherst, MA 01003

Harris Rhodes List
Box 142
La Veta, CO 81055
(719) 742 3146

ShoWhat *(Arizona shows)*
Doug Hawkins
3015 W. Pierce St.
Phoenix, AZ 85009

Southern Arts and Crafts (SAC)
PO Box 159
Bogalusa, LA 70429

Sunshine Artists Audit Book
1700 Sunset Dr.
Longwood, FL 32750-9697

The Crafts Fair Guide
Box 5508
Mill Valley, CA 94942

The Crafts Report
PO Box 1992
Wilmington, DE 19899

Appendix D: Wholesale Shows

American Craft Enterprises
PO Box 10
New Paltz, NY 12561
(800) 527-3844 (914) 883 6100

American Craft Marketing
Box 480
Slate Hill, NY 10973
(914) 355-2400

American Memories
Box 249
Decatur, MI 49045

Americana Sampler
Box 160020
Nashville, TN 37216
(615) 227-2080

AMC Trade Shows
1933 S. Broadway, Suite 111
Los Angeles, CA 90007
(213) 747-3488

Atlanta Merchandise Mart
Suite 2200, 240 Peachtree St. NW
Atlanta, GA 30303
(404) 220-3000

Beckman Shows
PO Box 27337
Los Angeles, CA 90027
(213) 962 5424

CMC, Fashion Accessory Expo
200 Connecticut Ave.
Norwalk, CT 06856
(203) 852-0500

Contemporary Crafts Market
777 Kapiolani Blvd, Suite 2820
Honolulu, HI 96813
(808) 422-7362

Charlotte Merchandise Mart
2500 E. Independence Blvd.
Charlotte, NC 28205
(704) 377-5881

Dallas Market Center
2100 Stemmons Freeway
Dallas, TX 75207
(214) 655-6100

George Little Management Co.
2 Park Avenue, Suite 1100
New York, NY 10016
(212) 686 6070

The Heritage Market
Box 389
Carlisle, PA 17013
(717) 249 9404

Int'l. Fashion Boutique Show
100 Well Ave.
Newton, MA 02159
(617) 964-5100

Karel Exposition Management
Box 19-1217
Miami Beach, FL 33119
(305) 534-7469

Market Square Wholesale Shows
PO Box 220
Newville, PA 17241
(717) 776 6989

Merchandise Mart & Apparel Center
Chicago, IL 60654
(312) 527-4141

NEOCON
Suite 470, The Merchandise Mart
222 Merchandise Mart Plaza
Chicago, IL 60654
(312) 527-7600

Offinger Management
Box 2188
Zanesville, OH 43702
(614) 452-2552

South Eastern Exhibitions
805 Parkway
Gatlinburg, TN 37738
Tradeshow & Exhibit Manager
1150 Yale St., Suite 12
Santa Monica, CA 90403

Wendy Rosen Shows
3000 Chestnut Ave., Suite 300
Baltimore, MD 21211
(301) 889 2933

Western Exhibitors
2181 Greenwich St.
San Francisco, CA 94121
(415) 346 6666

Appendix E: Advertising Media for Handwovens and Other Crafts

Access Fashion
Access Marketing
126 Fifth Ave.
New York, NY 10011   (212) 691 7100

Distribution: 1,000 copies to fashion firms, 5,000 copies to buyers at specialty stores and high-end boutiques, 10,000 copies to book stores. Lots of full color photo ads featuring wearable art, women's and men's wear and accessories.

American Craft Magazine
American Craft Council (ACC)
72 Spring St.
NY, NY 10012

Surveys and analyzes aesthetic and technical trends. Advertising available. Also contains extensive calendar listings of craft events. Subscription comes with membership in the ACC.

Art Vue
270 Lafayette, #1201
New York, NY 10012

All media slide registry for corporate clients. Send up to 20 slides, price list, resume and SASE for return of slides.

The Guild: The Architects Source of Artists and Artisans: Provides list of art consultants and artist reps by state; mural and sculpture artists.

The Guild: The Designer's Reference Book of Artists: Includes furniture, rugs, textiles, quilts, fiber, paper, mixed media, accesories, baskets and more.

The Guild
Kraus Sikes
228 State St.
Madison, WI 53703   (800) 969 1556

Distribution: 8,000 copies to interior designers, architects, art consultants, and public art agencies.

NICHE Magazine
The Rosen Agency
3000 Chestnut Ave., Suite 300
Baltimore, MD 21211
(301) 889 2933

Features craftspersons and their work, ideas for store management and information on The Rosen Agency Shows. Advertising available. Distribution: 25,000 buyers attending Rosen shows

Portfolio of American Crafts
GLM Publications
215 Lexington Avenue, Suite 1901
New York, NY 10016
(212) 532 0651

Select Homes and Food Magazine
2300 Yonge St
Toronto, Ontario M4P 3C4
Canada

Seeks craftspersons making home accessories. Publishes selected profiles of artists.

The Crafts Report
Box 1992
Wilmington, DE 19899

Publishes special sections previewing some of the major trade shows for craftspersons. Advertising available. Also features articles of importance to crafts business in the monthly edition. Distribution: retail buyers, craftspersons

Sampler Publications
707 Kautz Rd.
St. Charles, IL 60174

Industry Foundation Member's Directory, American Society of Interior Decorators, 608 Massachusetts Ave. NE, Washington, DC 20002-6006

Appendix F: Periodicals, Catalogs & Computer Software

Accessories Today
200 S. Main St.
High Point, NC 27261

Accessory Merchandising
408 Olive St.
St. Louis, MO 63102

American Artist
1515 Broadway
NY, NY 10036

American Craft Magazine
72 Spring St.
New York, NY 10012

Architectural Digest
5900 Wilshire Blvd.
Los Angeles, CA 90036

Artforum
65 Bleeker St., 13 Flr.
NY, NY 10012

Collector's News
PO Box 156
Grundy Center, IA 50638

Craft News/Ontario Crafts Council
35 McCaul St.
Toronto, Ontario M5T 1V7
Canada

The Crafts Report
PO Box 1992
Wilmington, DE 19899

Fiber Arts
50 College St.
Asheville, NC 28801

Gift Reporter
215 Lexington Ave., Suite 1901
NY, NY 10016

Gifts and Decorative Accessories
51 Madison Ave.
NY, NY 10010

Handwoven
201 E. Fourth St.
Loveland, CO 80537

Heddle
Box 1906
Bracebridge, Ontario P0B 1C0
Canada

Home Income Reporter
15 Brunswick Lane
Wilmingboro, NJ 08046

Interior Design
249 W. 17th St.
NY, NY 10011

Interiors
1515 Broadway, 39th Floor
NY, NY 10036

Journal for Weavers, Spinners & Dyers
38 Sandown Dr.
Hereford HR4 9LU
England

LDB Interior Textiles
370 Lexington Ave.
NY, NY 10017

Metropolitan Home
750 3rd Ave.
NY, NY 10017

National Arts Placement Newsletter
1916 Association Dr.
Reston, VA 22091
(703) 860-8000

National Home Business Report
Box 2137
Naperville, IL 60567

Ornament
PO Box 2349
San Marcos, CA 92079

Scandinavian Weaving Magazine
Glimakra Looms
1304 Scott St.
Petaluma, CA 94954

Sew News
PO Box 1790
Peoria, IL 61656

Shuttle Spindle & Dyepot
120 Mountain Avenue, B101
Bloomfield, CT 06002

Surface Design Journal
PO Box 20799
Oakland, CA 94620

Teaching for Learning
(newsletter for fiber arts teachers)
511 Hahaione St., #18-C
Honolulu, HI 96825

The Weaver's Friend
C/O Janet Meany
5672 North Shore Dr.
Duluth, MN 55804
(newsletter for rag rug weavers)

Threads
63 S. Main St.
Newtown, CT 06470

Tradeshow & Exhibit Manager
1150 Yale St., Suite 12
Santa Monica, CA 90403

Tradeshow & Exhibits Schedule
633 Third Avenue
New York, NY 10017

Weaver's
PO Box 1525
Sioux Falls, SD 57101-1525

Women's Wear Daily
7 East 12 St.
NY, NY 10003

Women Artist News
PO Box 3304
Grand Central Station
NY, NY 10163

Catalogs of Weaving, Textile and Craft marketing Books

Dos Tejedoras
Fiber Arts Publications
757 Raymond Ave., #300
St. Paul, MN 55114

Fiberworks Publications
PO Box 49770
Austin, TX 78765

Flower Valley Press
Box 645
Rockville, MD 20848

Handweavers Guild of America
Publications Department
120 Mountain Ave., B101
Bloomfield, CT 06002

Interweave Press
306 N. Washington Ave.
Loveland, CO 80537
(303) 669-7672

Lark Books
50 College St.
Asheville, NC 28801
(704) 253-0467

Lois Ericson
Box 5222
Salem, OR 97304

Robin & Russ Handweavers
533 N. Adams St.
McMinnville, OR

Straw Into Gold
3006 San Pablo
Berkeley, CA 94702

Sullivan Publications
1134 Montego Rd. West
Jacskonville, FL 32216

Unicorn Books
1304 Scott St.
Petaluma, CA 94954
(707) 762-3362

Virginia West
2809 Grasty Woods Ln.
Baltimore, MD 21208

Wooden Porch Books
Box 262
Middlebourne, WV 26149

Computer Software Suppliers

AVL Looms
601 Orange St.
Chico, CA 95928

Compucrafts
PO Box 326
Lincoln Ctr., MA 01773

Dini Cameron
8469 Franktown Rd., RR #3
Ashton, Ontario K0A 1B0, Canada

Fiberworks PCW
27 Suffolk West
Guelph, Ontario N1H 2H9, Canada

Joyce Peck, Amiga Desktop Weaving
Box 1051
Qualicum Beach, B.C. V0R 2T0
Canada

Lois Larson
25 Montcalm Ave.
Camrose, Alberta T4V 2K9, Canada

Maple Hill Software
Plainfield, VT 05667

Mindspun
RD2, Box 710
Andover, NJ 07821

PC Software & Supply
Rte. 1, Box 219H
South Sioux City, NE 68776

PsL (Public Software Library)
PO Box 35705
Houston, TX 77235

Swiftweave
PO Box 67
Crystal Bay, MN 55323

Appendix G: Weaving and Craft Schools

Appalachian Center for Crafts
Box 430, Rt. 3
Smithville, TN 37166

Arrowmont School
PO Box 567
Gatlinburg, TN 37738

Brookfield Craft Center
PO Box 122
Brookfield, CT 06804

Cooperstown Textile School
PO Box 455
Cooperstown, NY 13326

Coupeville Arts Center
Box 171
Coupeville, WA 98239

Elkhorn Mountains School
S.R. Box165
Clancy, MT 59634

Fashion Inst. of Technology
7th Ave. at 27th St.
New York, NY 10001

Fletcher Farm School
RR 1, Box 1041
Ludlow, VT 05149

Great Divide
Weaving School, Box 1
Divide, CO 80814

Harrisville Designs
Harrisville, NH 03450

Heritage Handweaving
Rt.3, Box 3086
Orland, CA 95963

Horizons
374 Old Montague Rd.
Amherst, MA 01002

John Campbell Folk School
Brasstown, NC 28902

The Looms
154 High St.
Mineral Point, WI 53565

Loom Shed Weaving School
14301 State Rt. 58
Oberlin, OH 44074

Marshfield School of Weaving
Plainfield, VT 05667

Mendocino Art Center
45200 Little Lake St.
Mendocino, CA 95460

Oregon School of Arts & Crafts
8245 SW Barnes Rd.
Portland, OR 97225

Penland School
Penland, NC 28765

Peters Valley Craft Center
19 Kuhn Rd.
Layton, NJ 07851

Philadelphia College of Textiles
School House Lane
Philadelphia, PA 19144

Saunderstown Weaving School
PO Box 517
Saunderstown, RI 02874

Sievers School of Fiber Arts
Tulip Lane
Washington Isle, WI 54246

Southern Illinois University at
Edwardsville, Art & Design Dpt
Edwardsville, IL 62026

Skidmore College
Saratoga Springs, NY 12866

Southwest Craft Center
300 Augusta St.
San Antonio, TX 78205

Spin & Weave
3054 N. First Ave.
Tucson, AZ 85719

Studio Gaustad
11178 Upper Previtali
Jackson, CA 95642

Taos Institute of Arts
PO Box 1389
Taos, NM 87571

Textile Arts Centre
916 W. Diversey Parkway
Chicago, IL 60614

The River Farm
Rt. 1, Box 401
Timberville, VA 22853

The Weaver's School
Rt.1
Fayette, MO 65248

The Weaving School
126 N. Church St.
West Chester, PA 19380

Tousand Islands Craft School
314 John St.
Clayton, NY 13624

Vermont State Craft Center
Middlebury, VT 05753

Worcester Center for Crafts
25 Sagamore Rd.
Worcester, MA 01605

Bibliography of Recommended Reading

American Council for the Arts Publications, 1285 Avenue of the Americas, 3rd Floor, New York, NY 10019 (800) 321-4510

How to Survive and Prosper as an Artist by Carol Michels

Supporting Yourself as an Artist by Deborah Hoover

The Artist's Survival Manual by Toby Klayman and Cobbett Steinberg

National Directory of Arts Internships

The Business of Being an Artist by Daniel Grant

Buyers and Sales Reps Lists

The Official Museum Directory by the American Association of Museums (see your library reference section)

Unique Programs, PO Box 9910, Marina del Rey, CA 90295. Their lists include over 1,000 galleries, 240 competitions, 260 museums and universities, 188 art publishers, 320 corporate collectors, 710 interior designers, 750 architects, 100 department stores and hotels. List prices range from $27 to $45 each.

ArtNetwork, 13284 Rices Crossing Rd., Renaissance, CA 95962 (800) 383-0677. Over 30 different mailing lists of artworld professionals including architects, designers, design centers, corporations collecting art, and many more. Average price of each list is $65 per 1,000 names.

ARTnews International Directory of Corporate Art Collections from Business Committee for the Arts, 1775 Broadway, NY, NY 10019.

Karen Gamow, Shops List
14618 Tyler Foote Rd.
Nevada City, CA 95959

Directory of Craft Shops/Galleries by Front Room Publishers, PO Box 1541, Clifton, NJ 07015

Directory of Wholesale Reps for Craft Professionals by Northwoods Publ.

Computers

Software for Weavers...A Resource, Lois Larson, 25 Montcalm Ave., Camrose, Alberta T4V 2K9 Canada

Computer Wimp No More by John Bear, Ph.D. (Ten Speed Press)

Design

Designing with Natural Forms by Natalie d'Arbeloff (Watson-Guptill)

Itten: The Elements of Color by Faber Birren (Van Nostrand Reinhold, 1970)

Fiberarts Design Book by Lark Books

Designing for Weaving: A Study Guide for Drafting, Design and Color by Carol Kurtz (Interweave Press, 1985)

Principles of Two Dimensional Design by Wucius Wong (Van Nostrand Reinhold Co., 1972)

The Enjoyment and Use of Color by Walter Sargent (Dover Publications, 1964)

Surface Design for Fabric by Richard Proctor and Jennifer Lew (Univ. of Washington Press, 1985)

The Textile Design Book by Karin Jerstorp and Eva Kohlmark (Lark Books)

Color and Fiber by Patricia Lambert, Barbara Staepelaere, and Mary Fry (Schiffer Publishing, West Chester, PA)

Color Trends, 8037 9th NW, Seattle, WA 98117. $62 + $3 ship.

Finishing Techniques

Finishes in the Ethnic Tradition by Suzanne Baizerman and Karen Searle. (Dos Tejedoras, 1978)

The Techniques of Rug Weaving and *Rug Weaving Techniques* by Peter Collingwood (Interweave Press)

Finishing Touches for the Handweaver by Virginia West (Interweave Press, 1988)

To the Finish by Lura Jim Bogdanor, 23 Cardigan Dr., St. Louis, MO 63135

Ashley's Book of Knots by Clifford Ashley (Doubleday)

General Reference

Textile Arts Index: 1950-1987 by Sayde Tune Wilson, Ruth Davidson Jackson (Tungstede Press, 212 Vaughn's Gap Rd., Nashville, TN 37205)

The Tapestry Handbook by Carol Russell (Lark Books)

Textiles As Art by Laurence Korwin (Korwin Design, 1990)

The Art Fabric: Mainstream by Mildred Constantine and Jack Lenor Larsen (Van Nostrand Reinhold)

Legal Help for Arts and Crafts

Business Forms and Contracts (In Plain English) for Craftspeople and *The Law (in Plain English) for Craftspeople* by Leonard DuBoff (Madronna Publishers)

Making it Legal: A Law Primer for Authors, Artists and Craftspeople by Martha Blue (Northland)

Legal Guide for the Visual Artist by Tad Crawford (Allworth)

Licensing Art & Design by Caryn Leland (Allworth)

Business &Legal Forms for Fine Artists by Tad Crawford (Allworth)

Volunteer Lawyers for the Arts publishes a catalog of legal advise books useful for craftspersons. Write for their catalog at VLA, 1 East 53 Street, 6th Floor, NY, NY 10022.

Photography and Lay-out

Looking Good In Print by Roger Parker (Ventana Press)

Photographing Your Craft Work by Steve Meltzer (Madrona Publishers, 1986)

Photographing Your Artwork by Russell Hart (Allworth Press)

Directory of Book Printers by John Kremer (Ad-Lib Publications, 1990)

Small Business Resources

Small Time Operator, How To Start Your Own Small Business, Keep Your Books, Pay Your Taxes, And Stay Out Of Trouble! by Bernard Kamoroff, C.P.A.

Guerilla Marketing, Secrets For Making Big Profits From Your Small Business by Jay Conrad Levinson

SBA Loans, A Step-By-Step Guide byPatrick O'Hara, Ph.D. (Wiley)

Creative Cash by Barbara Brabec, P.O.Box 2137, Naperville, IL 60567

Homemade Money by Barbara Brabec, P.O.Box 2137, Naperville, IL 60567

Anatomy of a Business Plan by Linda Pinson and Jerry Jinnett

Recordkeeping: The Secret to Growth and Profit by Linda Pinson & Jerry Jinnett (Out of Your Mind . . .)

Government Giveaways for Entrepreneurs by Matthew Lesko (Info, USA)

International Directory of Resources for Artisans by the Crafts Center, 1001 Connecticut Ave. NW, Suite 925, Washington, DC 20036.

Networking by Jessica Lipnack & Jeffrey Stamps

The Owner's and Manager's Market Analysis Workbook For Small to Moderate Retail and Service Establishments by Wayne Lemmon

Color Me Beautiful Make-up by Carol Jackson.

The Foundation Grants Index and *Foundation Fundamentals: A Guide for Grantseekers* by The Foundation Center (800) 424-9836

The Cooperative Approach to Crafts by Jan Halkett, William Seymour, and Gerald Ely, FREE from: U.S. Dept. of Agriculture, Agricultural Cooperative Service, Washington, DC 20250

How to Put On a Great Craft Show; First Time and Every Time by Dianne and Lee Spiegel, from FairCraft Publishing, (415) 924-3259

The Arts Festival Work Kit by Pam Korza and Dian Magie, (413) 545-2360.

The Whole Work Catalog, 1515 23rd St., Boulder, CO 80306. $1

The Work-at-Home Sourcebook, Arden. Check your library, bookstore or The Whole Work Catalog.

Weaving for the church market

Textiles for Today's Church by Roselyn Hahn, 706 Meadowbrook SE, Warren, OH 44484

Weaving as an Art Form: A Personal Statement by Theo Moorman (Schiffer Publishing,1986)

Glossary

A

account: any record of a business transaction.

accounts payable: money you owe to a business or individual for goods or services you have received but not yet paid for.

accounts receivable: money owed to a business for goods or services that have been delivered but not yet paid for.

assets: the valuable resources, properties and property rights owned by an individual or business, including accounts receivable.

B

bad debt: money owed to you that you cannot collect, such as returned checks you cannot collect on.

balance sheet: itemized statement which lists the total assets and the total liabilities of a business to portray its net worth at any given moment.

bookkeeping: the systemized process of recording business transactions into the accounting records.

breakeven: the point at which the business will neither make a profit not incur a loss; the point of activity when total revenue equals total expenses.

budget: a financial plan to control spending.

C

capital: funds necessary to start, operate or expand a business.

capital equipment: equipment used to manufacture a product, provide a service, or to sell, store, and deliver merchandise. Such equipment will not be sold in the normal course of business, but will be used and worn out or consumed in the course of business.

cash flow: the actual movement of cash within a business; cash inflow minus cash outflow.

collateral: something of value given or held as a pledge that a debt or obligation will be fulfilled.

contract: an agreement regarding mutual responsibilities between two or more parties.

cooperative: a business in which the employees own, operate, and manage the business. Profits are distributed based on the amount of time each owner-employer has invested in the business rather than the amount of capital investment of each owner.

corporation: an organization of persons, either actual individuals or legal entities, legally bound together to form a business enterprise; an artificial legal entity created by government grant.

co-signers: joint signers of a loan agreement, pledging to meet the obligations in case of default.

cost of goods sold: the direct cost to the business owner of those items which will then be sold to their customers. Cost of goods does not include other indirect costs of being in business like rent, utilities, and so on.

credit: monies received.

D

debt: that which is owed; refers to borrowed funds from your own resources, or from individuals, banks, or institutions.

default: failure to pay a debt or meet an obligation.

depreciation: a decrease in value through age, wear or deterioration. Depreciation is a normal expense of doing business regulated by tax laws.

E

entrepreneur: an innovator of a business enterprise who recognizes opportunities to introduce a new product, process or improved organization, and who raises the money and organizes an operation to exploit the opportunity.

equity: the owner's investment in the business; carries with it a share of ownership, a stake in the profits and a say in how the business is managed.

F

financial statement: document that shows the financial condition of a business or individual.

G

gross profit: calculated by subtracting cost of goods sold from net sales. The difference between the selling price and the cost of an item.

guarantee: a pledge by a third party to repay a loan in the event the borrower can't.

I

income statement: a financial document that shows how much money came in and how much money was paid out.

interest: the cost of borrowing money.

inventory: the materials owned and held by a business intended either for internal consumption or for sale. Includes new material, intermediate products and parts, work-in-progress, and finished goods.

L

lease: long term rental agreement.

liability insurance: risk protection for actions for which a business is liable.

license: formal permission to do something. Licenses are granted for such things as producing and selling items with someone else's design or trademark.

liquidity: ability of a business to meet its financial responsibilities. The degree of readiness with which assets can be converted into cash without a loss.

M

management: the art of conducting and supervising a business.

market niche: a group of customers for which what you have to offer is particularly suitable.

marketing: all the activities involved in the buying and selling of a product or service.

merchandise: goods bought and sold in a business.

N

net worth: the total value of an entity or individual in financial terms. Net worth is calculated by subtracting what you owe from what you own.

O

operating (indirect) costs: expenses incurred to do business like salaries, rent, electricity, telephone, etc.

P

partnership: a legal relationship created by the voluntary association of two or more persons who share responsibilities, resources, profits and liabilities.

principal: 1) the amount of money borrowed in a debt agreement; or 2) the owner of a business

pro forma: a projection or estimate of what may result in the future from actions in the present. A pro forma financial statement is one that shows how the actual operations of a business will turn out if certain assumptions are realized.

profit: the excess of the selling price over all costs and expenses incurred in making a sale.

profit margin: the difference between the selling price and costs.

profit and loss statement: a list of the total amount of sales (revenues) and total costs (expenses). The difference between revenues and expenses is the profit or loss.

R

revenue: total sales during a stated period.

retail: selling direct to the consumer.

S

sales representative (rep): an independent salesperson who direct their efforts to selling your products to others but is not an employee of your company. Sales reps often represent more than one product line form more than one company and usually work on commission.

share (stock): one of the equal parts into which the ownership of a corporation is divided.

sole proprietorship: a type of business organization in which one individual owns the business. Legally the owner is the business and personal assets are typically exposed to liabilities of the business.

spreadsheet: generic term for a computer program which allows you to easily record and manipulate numeric data. In business they are used for bookkeeping, preparing financial statements, and forecasting sales.

S corporation: a corporation which has elected by consent of its stockholders not to pay any corporate tax on its income and instead, to have the shareholders pay personal taxes on it, even though it may not have been distributed to them.

T

target market: the specific individuals, identified by socio-economic, demographic, and interest characteristics, who are the most likely potential customers for the goods and services of a business.

terms of sale: the conditions concerning payment for a purchase.

trade credit: credit which is given to you by a supplier. Trade credit is generally accompanied by a trade discount from the price which you receive if you pay your bill early.

V

venture capital: money invested in enterprises that do not have access to traditional sources of capital like banks. Venture capital is usually associated with high risk, high pay-off businesses.

volume: an amount or quantity of business; the total a business sells over a period of time.

W

wholesale: selling for resale

working capital: the cash needed to keep the business running from day to day. Working capital is calculated by subtracting current liabilities from current assets.

Index

Bookshelf

Check your library for these valuable business references. Titles listed here may also be ordered directly from Warm Snow Publishers, Box 75, Torreon, Nm 87061, Use the order form following.

Weaving Profits, *How to Make Money Selling Your Handwovens or Any Other Crafts* by James Dillehay

Hailed as "the blueprint for success in the crafts industry," Weaving Profits is the only crafts marketing guide that specifically helps weavers and fiber artists with their special business needs. Contains sixteen chapters covering over 180 subjects on selling handwovens, plus extensive appendixes of over 280 resources useful to fiber craftspersons. The Bookwatch calls it "Invaluable -- and not just for weavers alone." 8 1/2 x 11", 198 pages, softcover, $19.95.

Small Time Operator, *How to Start Your Own Small Business, Keep Your Books, Pay Your Taxes, and Stay Out of Trouble!* by Bernard Kamoroff, C.P.A., (Bell Springs Press)

This classic business guide is a technical manual written in an understandable, non-technical style. It includes complete, readable information to start and successfully operate any small business including: permits, licenses, insurance, bank accounts, financing, bookkeeping, taxes, employees, partnerships, corporations, and much more. Over 450,000 copies sold and in use. 8 1/2 x 11", 192 pages, softcover, $14.95.

Recordkeeping: The Secret to Growth and Profit by Linda Pinson & Jerry Jinnett (Out of Your Mind and Into the Marketplace Publishers)

A comprehensive guide for setting up, analyzing, and understanding all aspects of business recordkeeping. The reader is led through the logical sequence of developing a recordkeeping system and is shown the interrelationship of records, statements, and tax accounting. With extensive worksheets, examples and index. The authors were chosen by the U.S. Small Business Administration to write the agency's new business plan publication. 8 1/2 x 11", 158 pages, softcover, $17.00

Creative Cash, *How to Sell Your Crafts, Needlework, Designs & Know-how* by Barbara Brabec

An entertaining and well-rounded education in the how-to's and realities of making a part- or full-time living from crafts or needlework. Profiles of craft businesses and examples of success techniques plus 200 art/craft marketing resources. Includes beginning legal and financial information plus help on copyrighting your designs and getting them published. 8 1/2 x 11", 200 pages, softcover, $16.95.

Bookshelf Order Form

Check your library for these valuable business references. Titles listed here may also be ordered directly from Warm Snow Publishers, Box 75, Torreon, Nm 87061, Use the order form here. All books are guaranteed, if you aren't satisfied for any reason, return the books for a full refund, no questions asked.

When you order three books (any titles) or more, you get 10% off the total retail price!

Order from: Warm Snow Publishers

                Bookshelf, Box 75

                Torreon, NM 87061

Please send me:

__ copies of **WEAVING PROFITS** $19.95

__ copies of **Small Time Operator** $14.95

__ copies of **Recordkeeping: The Secret to Growth & Profit** $17.00

__ copies of **Creative Cash** $16.95

total _____

deduct 10% when ordering 3 or more _____

shipping (add $3.50 for 1st book, $1 for each additional) _____

Enclosed is my check for: _____

YOUR NAME _____

ADDRESS _____

CITY, STATE, ZIP _____